To Marty & [illegible]

whose friendship

I treasure —

I have the best

Congressman in the

country, and he's

luckier - he has

Sylvia.

[illegible]

Sept. 12, 2004

The Uncivil War

THE UNCIVIL WAR

How a New Elite
Is Destroying Our Democracy

DAVID LEBEDOFF

TAYLOR TRADE PUBLISHING
Lanham • New York • Dallas • Boulder • Toronto • Oxford

Published by Taylor Trade Publishing
An imprint of The Rowman & Littlefield Publishing Group, Inc.
4501 Forbes Boulevard, Suite 200
Lanham, Maryland 20706

Distributed by National Book Network

Library of Congress Cataloging-in-Publication Data

Lebedoff, David.
    The uncivil war : how a new elite is destroying our democracy / David M. Lebedoff.
        p. cm.
    ISBN: 1-58979-151-7
    1. Elite (social sciences)—United States. 2. Social classes—Political aspects—United
States. 3. United States—Politics and government—1989. I. Title.
HN90.E4 L43 2004
305.5'0973—dc22   2003020858

∞™ The paper used in this publication meets the minimum requirements of
American National Standard for Information Sciences—Permanence of
Paper for Printed Library Materials, ANSI/NISO Z39.48–1992.
Manufactured in the United States of America.

For Judy and Lisa

PERMISSIONS

CONTENTS

Contents

BACKWORD

I know, I know. The introduction to a book is supposed to be called the "foreword," but in this case a little history is in order. Before we get going, we should look for a minute in the rearview mirror.

Let's go back forty years. That's just the right distance to produce a golden glow, though in fact most people are better off today. They're better off materially (though not necessarily in comparison with others), and many millions enjoy much greater opportunity and respect than they did in the hallowed days of Camelot. In many ways, we are both a stronger and more sensitive nation than we have ever been.

But some things are not better today—for anyone. Our political system has sickened and died. Our sense of community is almost a memory. Our general culture is no longer general, and its level is sinking fast. The erosion of civility is shocking. All the progress that we've made in other areas, progress of which we should be proud, cannot excuse or disguise the new loss of community or the unresponsiveness of government.

How did all this happen? It didn't happen overnight. In my own case, the outbreak afflicting our society became unavoidably visible about thirty years ago. I wasn't sure at first, but I had the advantage of being close to where the disease first spread. I had spent about ten years, starting in 1966, very much involved in political activity on behalf of candidates in the Democratic–Farmer–Labor Party in my home state, Minnesota. The state had two strong political parties back then, broad based and issue oriented, but the deadly virus had already begun to work on them. You could see the change, not day to day, but by the early 1970s a system that had been widely praised as a national model of honesty and effectiveness was obviously ailing and getting steadily worse. Soon there was no mistaking a pandemic. What was the problem?

Answering this was made much easier simply by looking around. The people involved in politics were changing. The more one heard about the increase in "activism," the more the number of those who had been politically active actually shrank. Fewer people were in the process, and those who arrived seemed noticeably different from the far greater number who had left. Different in attitude, outlook, tone, goals, behavior, and appearance. It was clear that one group was being displaced by another. It was clear that the political process was dramatically changing. It became increasingly evident that these things were related and why.

In 1978, I published an article in *Esquire* called "The Dangerous Arrogance of the New Elite." I pointed out a connection between the spreading affliction and the fanaticism of a new class whose self-identity was based on measured intelligence. I called this class the New Elite, and everyone else the Left Behinds. At the heart of the connection between the new class and a new set of problems was the fact that the New Elite had ceased to believe in majority rule. So it was busily cutting the wires between the people and their government.

I made it clear that the doctrine of majority rule includes, indeed requires, the preservation of even the most unpopular minority rights that are expressly protected by a written constitution. But strengthened by that exception, majority rule remained the best hope for a land of opportunity for all, and that hope was being severely threatened by the growth of a new class.

This article generated a certain amount of attention, and I expanded it into a book, *The New Elite*, which was published in 1981.

The reaction to the book surprised me. The reviews were very favorable, but they appeared only in conservative publications. I was then what was known as a moderate Democrat. Why did *National Review* and the Heritage Foundation applaud my thesis and everyone else ignore it? My book was not partisan. It was an impassioned plea for return to majority rule. What was so conservative about majority rule?

Well, that's really not the right question. What the reviewers were interested in was why the New Elite was so liberal. The new class that I had defined looked to conservatives exactly like the enemy they'd been fighting most recently.

This was somewhat beside the point. The New Elite was "liberal" at its inception, and its efforts to dismantle our majoritarian structures were originally confined to the Democratic Party. But aha! A virus so virulent soon spreads. Now both parties are on life support, the valves guarded by extremists.

The real battle that has turned this country into opposing and very hostile camps is not between conservatives and liberals. It is between those who believe in majority rule and those who believe in rule by experts. It is between those who rely primarily on experience and those who rely primarily on theories.

Yes, there is some correlation between the political parties—enough to make the red and the blue of recent election maps a recognizable metaphor for our subject.

But our subject is not really political—or at least not partisan. The division of America is not between liberal programs and conservative programs, or big government and small government. The New Elite has no program. Its only real policy goal is that all policy be made by members of the New Elite. The voters sense this, and so every election now is really about candidate identification. A great many people want to know which contender is most likely to be a member of the New Elite, so that they then can vote for the other one. (The most recent example of the majoritarian backlash is the gubernatorial victory of Arnold Schwarzenegger. Like the majority of California and American voters, he was somewhat liberal on social issues and more conservative in fiscal matters—which means that he could not have been endorsed by either party.) The Bush–Kerry race, its outcome unknown at this writing, will be greatly affected by the new polarity that now marks all elections.

When *The New Elite* was written, there were few well-known examples to illustrate these points. But time has solved that problem. All the hapless headlines of the past few decades, all the seismic convulsions from impeachment to Enron, are merely inevitable facets of the new class ascendancy. However disparate may appear the unfolding horrors in our national life, they're usually part of the same problem. There are enough examples now to see that pattern. Perhaps the best example so far is the presidential election of 2000, which is covered in the first chapter of this book, "The Perfect Storm."

The next few chapters define the birth of a new class and are adapted from *The New Elite*. More than twenty years ago, they set forth the thesis of what I thought was going on. The rest of the book relies on what has happened since then, why everything that happens, from elections to movies, seems to be getting worse—the streams that have become a torrent.

And of course a cast of characters now exists that formerly was impossible even to imagine. That cast raucously struts the stage, though with no concern whatever for the audience. The pages of this book are peopled with actors adhering all too publicly to a script of their own devising. Though now they need no introduction to the reader, it may still be helpful to see how they got their parts.

PART ONE

THE NEW ELITE

ONE

The Perfect Storm:
The Bush/Gore Race in 2000

Al Gore is a Harvard man. George W. Bush went to Yale. Their preparatory schools were also exceptionally elite—Bush: Andover, Gore: St. Albans. Both had politically powerful fathers—one a president, the other a U.S. senator. Though Al Gore and George Bush would run for president as barefoot boys from Tennessee and Texas, those toes had been wiggled in country club pools.

They are both good family men. Each has a strong and intelligent wife and is widely regarded as a devoted parent. Both attend church regularly. Unlike most of their privileged contemporaries, each served, more or less, in the military.

Peas in a pod? Hardly. They are in fact the most dissimilar rivals ever to face off against one another in a presidential race. They are at the far opposite ends of the spectrum—the political spectrum now being defined in terms of new class warfare.

It is a war that began when intelligence came to be tested. Rewarding ability is of course highly desirable. But there is a tendency to reward not achievement but rather test scores. It is widely assumed that there is one single capacity called general intelligence and that it can be accurately measured. Many (not all) of those with high scores can't escape the feeling that since we know who the smartest people are, there is no longer any point in seeking the opinions of anyone else. Why should we let the majority rule?

Those who are the "we" in this question are the New Elite. Everyone else, regardless of intellect or income, is one of the Left Behinds. These are the groups who are at war. It is a strange war, with one side advancing only by stealth, and the other organized largely for defense.

The battlefields are cultural as well as political, but the clearest conflicts are usually national elections. For some time now, they've been heavily influenced by the new class war, but never more so than in the Bush/Gore contest.

Gore of course was the New Elite candidate and Bush the Left Behind.

And this is why Bush won.

He certainly didn't win on the issues. As the presidential race of 2000 grew nearer, the stars seemed in alignment for the Democrats. On issue after issue, the polls showed a clear majority favoring the policies of the party in office. On abortion, gun control, tax cuts, health care, tobacco regulation, and other issues, the numbers showed that the Republican positions were not shared by most Americans. When the Republicans came up with a popular new policy—such as welfare reform—it was swiftly stolen and completely co-opted by President Clinton, thereby turning the issue gap into a gorge.

Further, the economy was very, very strong. There was a book out about the Dow Jones average reaching 36,000. The market had in fact been going up so long and so high that perhaps there really was no ceiling. Unemployment was astonishingly low. All this would change, of course, but not before the presidential election.

There was, to be sure, a cloud over the personal life of the incumbent president. Though a clear majority had opposed his removal from office by impeachment, there was widespread public revulsion over all the tawdry revelations and a very understandable desire to change the channel. The vice president was stuck with his president's vice, the taint necessarily so.

Even so, the polls suggested that had the constitution permitted him to seek a third term, even *Clinton* could have survived the Clinton scandals. He probably would have clobbered Bush.

This is because Clinton was a magician. He didn't need smoke and mirrors. He could turn himself into anything. He had magic. So while embodying almost every characteristic and attitude of the New Elite, he could just stand there and face the populace and—poof!—he was someone else. He was one of them. It was almost like the movie *Men in Black,* where people were zapped with electronic wands and made to forget the alien secrets they had just observed.

Al Gore did not have a magic wand. He couldn't change into anything except earth tones. By election day, almost everyone (with the exception of Gore himself) knew who he was—he was the person who didn't know who he was.

He was the prototype of the New Elite. You can't get any closer to its essence, its embodiment, its very definition.

And that's why the 2000 campaign can be called the Perfect Storm. Because in the opposite corner was the champion of the Left Behinds. The choice had never been so remarkably clear. These weren't two leaders of opposing camps, these *were* the opposing camps. One couldn't invent two candidates who more precisely personified each side of the new class struggle.

Which is, as noted, why Bush won. Or, more accurately, why Gore lost. The Gore persona became increasingly defined as the campaign developed. The Bush persona did not. That came largely after 9/11. During the campaign, and right through election day, much of the voting public knew very little about George W. Bush.

Everyone knew that his father had been president. To get around the similarity of their names, the press took to calling the son "Dubya," for his middle initial W. "Dubya" sounded kind of Texan, and it reminded people that he was governor of Texas.

But six years earlier, he hadn't even held public office. His reviews as governor were largely favorable, but outside of Texas he continued to be known as his father's son and little else.

Much fun was made of the way he spoke. His speech was straightforward, but his sentences were disjointed and his syntax often a mess. This gave rise to the impression, in the opposition camp at least, that Dubya really wasn't very bright.

This was a mistake—in fact the classic mistake that the new class makes in judging candidates. Those who write about such things prefer candidates who sound like themselves—or as they think they sound, or want to sound, or sound after editing.

The political landscape is littered with the whitened bones of erudite commentators who underestimated candidates who didn't speak the way they spoke. Truman, Eisenhower, and Reagan were able to ascend history's ladder despite such denigration, and none required a Henry Higgins to do so.

But the word was out in many circles that Bush was pretty dumb. It was sneeringly noted that he had been a college cheerleader, that his friends were businessmen, that he had been part owner of a baseball team, that he wore cowboy boots, and that he spoke seldom, bluntly, and with a twang. When it was pointed out that Bush not only had a B.A. from Yale but an M.B.A. from Harvard, his detractors usually replied that it was easier to get into those places back then.

"Back then" was indeed a time that was ending just after George Bush was admitted to Yale. Dubya's father and grandfather had attended Yale. Of course, he would as well. But this was precisely the moment when college admissions swung from the old elite to the New Elite. Dubya squeezed in just before the family door was closed. From now on, SAT scores mattered much more than whether your grandfather was Senator Prescott Bush. Dubya's younger brothers, Governor Jeb and the rest, did not attend Yale.

The New Elite had already established a beachhead at Yale when Dubya was there. And he didn't like it. "Nothing illustrated Bush's alienation from this new world better than his hatred of Strobe Talbott, chairman of the *Yale Daily News,* Rhodes scholar, and meritocrat par excellence. Talbott irked Bush no end. To borrow the WASP term of art, Talbott, who would later become Clinton's foreign policy guru, was a 'grind,' a first-rate party pooper. To this day, the *New York Times* has reported, Bush still carps about him" (Franklin Foer, *New Republic,* February 5, 2001).

That was Bush. Now what about Gore? His Harvard years were marked by the same tectonic class shift that was rocking Yale. But in Gore's case, the change was welcome. Very welcome. He *loved* the New SAT Elite. In fact, it was the start of a lifelong infatuation. Many years later, with brilliant insight, Nicholas Lemann wrote in the July 31, 2000, issue of *The New Yorker* that Gore's book "'Earth in the Balance' is not so much the work of an intellectual as the work of someone immensely impressed by intellectualism and intellectuals, who occupy the venerated position for him that baseball heroes do for Bush."

And there you have it. The most important thing to know about the New Elite is that it is self-selected. It's the values you choose to side with. If you perceive, as Foer puts it, "merit not as brainpower but as 'character',", then, like Bush, you're a Left Behind. If your central value is brainpower itself, above all else, you are a member of the New Elite, the club to which Gore chose to belong.

It's all how you see yourself. And while the New Elite is supposedly based on "objective" test scores, there is nothing objective whatsoever about including oneself. Admission is shameless. If you think that it is a much better fraternity than DKE, then you just voted yourself in.

There is no admissions test; that's just for college. You don't even have to go to college to be in the New Elite. You just have to feel that you belong. Although if you plan to get along with your new friends, you've got to talk the talk and walk the walk.

Actually, the talking is more important than the walking. (With Left Behinds, the opposite is probably the case.) Look at how Gore talks. Then Bush.

The perfect contrast between the two appeared in an article by Tucker Carlson in the September 1999 issue of the now-defunct *talk* magazine, more than a year before the election. It refers to a profile of Gore by Louis Menand that had appeared in *The New Yorker.* "At one point," notes Carlson, "Gore waxes enthusiastic to Menand about the French philosopher Maurice Merleau–Ponty's *Phenomenology of Perception,* a work, Gore explains, that he found useful 'in cultivating a capacity for a more refined introspection that gave me better questions that ultimately led to a renewed determination to become involved with the effort to make things better.' As Menand points out, 'It is a little hard to imagine having this conversation with George W. Bush.'

"And it is," notes Carlson. "When I ask Bush to name something he isn't good at, there is no hesitation at all. 'Sitting down and reading a 500-page book on public policy or philosophy or something,' he says."

Carlson, a writer for the conservative *Weekly Standard,* was clearly delighted to quote both candidates. He saw at once that Gore's supposed erudition was not the slam dunk that Menand assumed. It was, in fact, a smoke alarm for the Left Behinds. For one thing, Gore speaks in social science prose. His statement would have been appalling enough had he written it out, but to actually *speak* like that, to use all these words to say, apparently, that a French writer made him think more clearly and therefore better able to do good, is stupefying.

Bush's response is equally telling. What counts most is that he said it. To deny that one's Energizer is a position paper is to invite the scorn of the New Elite—as Bush learned well at Yale. To give this answer in an interview is to extend, as Gore might phrase it, the middle digit to the New Elite.

Only a fool would suppose that Bush was endorsing stupidity. Politicians know that voters don't want stupid presidents. Nor was his a redneck's snarl against his betters. Yes, Yale and Harvard were easier to get into when he went there, but not *that* much easier. In point of fact, Bush's SAT scores were higher than Gore's—a fact about which only one of them gives a damn. As we have seen, it's all about self-selection. It isn't a question of who really is smarter than whom.

What's going on is something else entirely. Perhaps the best example comes from the Clinton years. While one does not readily make light of the very real pain endured in the Clinton White House after the suicide of Vince Foster, it is noteworthy that in recounting that tragedy, Hillary Clinton has told how they procured a number of books on grieving and passed them around within their circle. Perhaps these books really helped; one sincerely hopes so. But one essential difference between the New Elite and the Left Behinds is the difference between reading books on grieving and simply grieving.

The above sheds some light on Bush's disinclination to read "a 500-page book on public policy." He understands that *someone* in his administration has to read such books, but that his own job, choosing between policy alternatives, is more usefully linked to the application of core values than the analysis of transitory data.

The voters understand this. People respond to candidates who respond to people—not feeling their pain, but sharing their values. The voters don't want a president eager to test some untried theory with the quality of their lives— or indeed, with their lives. They want a president who agrees with Oliver Wendell Holmes that "a page of history is worth a volume of logic."

Holmes was a Left Behind, too, as well as perhaps our greatest jurist. Like Bush, though much more so, he was something of an aristocrat—a genuine Boston Brahmin. But his basic allegiance was not to an old elite—Holmes had passionate faith in the wisdom of the majority. As does Bush to a great extent, although the M.B.A. president also thinks highly of the managerial elite as well.

Class allegiance. It's what voters look for now, more than anything else. You have to listen to how people talk. How many words would it take Al Gore to say, "A page of history is worth a volume of logic"? Three pages? Even the most self-absorbed pedagogues know that obtuse expression will turn off an audience, which is why beltway commentators have learned a few folksy phrases with which to season their pedantry. ("That dog won't hunt" and "at the end of the day" seem to be the current favorites.)

But you really can't fake it. (Even Clinton didn't really fake it; he just had this magic trick of actually *being* the kind of person each audience wanted.) Bush is of course not really a cowboy, and he does indeed get more audience mileage out of his West Texas ranch than *The Phantom of the Opera* eked out of that chandelier, but symbols aside, he's still pretty much who he says he is. He's the embodiment of the Left Behinds, and the voters know it.

Of course, in electing him president, the voters had some help. Karl Rove has advised the younger Bush since before even the Texas gubernatorial campaign. As recounted by Franklin Foer:

> Rove insisted that [Bush] read the works of David Horowitz and Myron Magnet, both of whom accused intellectuals of unmooring society from its bedrock values. . . .

And when Rove began organizing Bush's presidential bid in the summer of 1998, he once again turned to Horowitz and Magnet, importing them to Austin to lecture the governor on the new class and the roots of cultural decay.

W. proved a receptive pupil. Horowitz's and Magnet's screeds against the intellectual elite jibed with his own brush with the destructive generation at Yale.

So. Not only was the Bush/Gore race a clear conflict between the New Elite and the Left Behinds, but *Bush knew it! Rove* knew it. They had *planned* for this. They were *counting* on the new class war to tip the election to Bush.

And it did. Though, God knows, just barely. But that's the point—the election was close enough that dangling chads and hanging judges could make a difference. It would never have been so close—not remotely—had the election not turned into the Gettysburg of the new class war.

It *wasn't* so close in the polls, at first. Gore had the lead. Not only was Bush still largely unknown to the public—what *was* known about him was often detrimental. When threatened by the very popular John McCain in the Republican primaries, for example, Bush scurried over to Bob Jones University to be publicly embraced by the religious right, on a campus that had banned interracial dating. The general public may prefer traditional values, but not *that* traditional. To emerge as its nominee, Bush had had to move closer to his party's extreme wing. The public is centrist. Moving toward the extreme of either party is damaging, especially in November.

Also, there is a threshold test for president, shared by almost everyone, and that threshold is competence. Not competence as Dukakis defined it—who is the "smarter" candidate—but whether a candidate is even minimally competent to do the job of governing.

A lot of people weren't sure about Bush. Everyone knew that Gore was a smarty-pants, and that cut both ways; but even those who hated his sense of superiority could not deny him a pass on the competence threshold test. Gore was achingly familiar with federal government. Bush didn't seem to be.

One problem with deliberately running as a Left Behind is that it is easier for some voters to think that you're dumb. These voters were appalled when, in response to a reporter's question, Bush failed to know the name of the president of Pakistan.

Having to come up with such information on demand is one of the stupider tests that the New Elite has come up with to prove who's "smarter"—as if the retentive capacities of support staff were suddenly more important than decisiveness based on values. In little more than a year, however, it became pretty clear that the capacity to win over as an ally the president of Pakistan was more important than previously having known his name.

Though hobbled by voters' doubts, Bush won the election. The electoral map immediately became famous—the Red and the Blue. "A Country Divided," headlined *Newsweek* on January 22, 2001: "The red and blue map of Election 2000 tells the story of two increasingly disparate nations: Democrats in metropolitan areas and Republicans in the vast open spaces."

But the blue and the red do not fundamentally stand for urban versus rural. They stand far more demonstrably for the opposing camps in the new class war. Members of the new class do indeed tend to move to cities, as we shall see, but the national schism is not really a matter of geography.

All that is left to be noted on the election of 2000 is the exceptional bitterness in the painful time between the overture of balloting and the Supreme Court finale. A bitterness that is with us still.

In the welter of invective after the final decision was reached, few voices from either side were restrained. A rare voice of calm and reason was that of Andrew Sullivan, writing as "TRB" in the December 25 issue of *The New Republic*, where he noted sadly the futility of Gore's ceaseless quest for selective recounts:

> In Gore's mind, which is an almost perfect incarnation of the rationalist world view, the truth was always out there, and there was a way to reach it. But this was a chimera. . . .
>
> In many aspects, this entire electoral ordeal has been a function of Gore's trying too hard. He should have done the simple things: run on his economic record, stuck to his New Democrat credentials, won his home state, conceded when he first lost, and followed the election rules in place on November 7. He did much more and ended up with much less. And the man who could barely string a sentence together, campaigned weakly, and retired to a ranch while Gore stayed surgically attached to his Palm Pilot won the prize. This will seem an irony to some, a lesson to others. Maybe Dubya was the truly smart one after all.

TWO

The Birth of a Class

It was time for Thomas to get married. He was almost eighteen, his father had died, and the patch of land was now his. He needed a wife to help with the work, to cook and sew and bear children. He needed a wife as much as he needed the sun and the rain and the protection of his feudal lord. He wanted companionship, too, and sex. His needs were urgent and could not be postponed.

The problem was finding a bride. In Thomas's limited world, there were three single women of marriageable age. One was sickly, one was strong, and one was beautiful. He married the one who was strong. There was really no other choice. The sickly woman could not work his poor land, and the beautiful one did not want to. She had other alternatives.

Thomas's bride was named Katherine. The couple got on very well, which is to say that even when not stupefied by labor they seldom fought with one another. He never regretted choosing her, nor did she regret being chosen by him. They seemed to be compatible.

Neither Thomas nor Katherine ever wondered who was smarter. Intelligence was not a factor in marital selection. There was no such thing as an IQ test. No one even suspected that intelligence could be measured. There would have been no point to such measurement. Intelligence was not related to one's station in life. There was no social or economic mobility. A person was born to a certain role and stayed there. Most people spent their lives on the land in harsh drudgery.

As it happened, Katherine was much the brighter of the two. Using the numerical scale with which we are familiar today, Thomas's IQ was 105 and Katherine's was 147. This means that Thomas's intelligence was very near average (100) and Katherine's was in the "genius" category. Neither suspected this disparity, for both were illiterate. Almost everyone was. The conditions of their lives did not recognize, let alone reward, Katherine's special gifts.

Thomas and Katherine lived in England in the twelfth century, but the circumstances of their union would have been much the same in Italy or Russia or China, in the Middle Ages or the Renaissance. From the dawn of time until the eighteenth century, the process of marital selection was very much the same. Spouses were chosen from the very small pool of those who happened to live nearby. They were chosen without regard to, and without any way of knowing, what their general intelligence might be.

Until fairly recently, intelligence was randomly scattered throughout the population. Almost all people were peasants, and that included most people with high IQs. Some members of the tiny ruling class were undoubtedly brighter than the average, just as some others most assuredly were not, but that class was so small that its composition could not affect the general distribution of intelligence throughout the total population.

By and large, intelligence had nothing to do with one's station in life. A genius comparable to Einstein could have died illiterate after a lifetime of serfdom in the fields. No one would have known of his ability, and no one would have cared.

Two biological truths remained constant throughout human history until the modern age: (1) intelligence was randomly distributed and (2) people mated without much regard to the intelligence of their marriage partners. The second truth ensured the continuity of the first. A man and a woman each with an IQ of 150 will very probably produce children who are brighter than average, but (also probably) not quite as bright as their parents. The tendency is for the offspring to move back toward (or up toward) the average. This is known as regression toward the mean. If one of the children has an IQ of 140 and marries someone with an IQ of 160, *their* child might have an IQ of 150. So if bright people continue to marry only bright people, their children will continue to be bright, and the principle of regression toward the mean can often be avoided.

But of course this did not happen. With regard to the matching of their IQs, people married just as arbitrarily as did Thomas and Katherine. Biologically, it was close to a purely random selection. It was extremely unlikely that any of Thomas's and Katherine's great-grandchildren would have IQs as high as Katherine's.

In the modern age, all of this changed. The change began only a few hundred years ago, but it has already altered irrevocably the patterns of human life on this planet. For the first time in history, intelligence is neither randomly distributed nor randomly transmitted.

Three factors account for this change. First, there is greater mobility now; the search for a spouse need not stop at the farm next door. After the Industrial Revolution, most people did not live on small, isolated farms but in cities and towns. Aldous Huxley observed (at the time, people thought he was jesting) that the most important invention in history was the bicycle, because it meant that a person could reach, and therefore choose, a spouse from several dozen possibilities rather than two or three.

This is not to say that people could marry whomever they wished. The young suitor of the eighteenth, nineteenth, and early twentieth centuries was still likely to confine his search to women of his own social and economic background. He may have been more interested in their physical appearance or their dowries than their minds, but the expansion of choice also permitted him to choose someone whose company he enjoyed. This was an important new factor in selection. If the couple shared the same interests and enjoyed each other's conversation, the chances were improved that their intelligence would be roughly the same.

Second, universal education has become the rule in the Western world. If everyone can read and write, everyone can be graded and tested. Children can be told precisely how smart they are supposed to be, and that information, coupled with the resultant self-image, can help determine the choice of a spouse.

The third—and by far the most important—factor is that, today, intellectual ability is rewarded. This is something very new in human history. Until very recently, real equality of opportunity did not exist. Now, by and large, one's ability *is* relevant to one's station in life, and people *can* rise to the level that their talent permits. The son of a cobbler is not necessarily destined to be a cobbler himself. He might be an accountant. And he might marry the daughter of a shopkeeper. People still tend to marry within their social and economic class, but membership in that class has come to depend more on measurable intelligence and less on circumstances of birth. A natural selection by ability has taken place.

The pace of this progress at first was very slow. Even in the United States during the early part of the twentieth century, intelligence generally remained randomly scattered throughout the population. Most people were members of what was called the working class; for them, equality of opportunity remained out of reach. It was still true that there were poor neighborhoods inhabited by many individuals of high general intelligence—whether they knew it or not—who spent their lives working in menial and low-paying jobs.

Over ensuing decades, however, the situation changed dramatically. Equality of opportunity for white Americans became the norm, not the exception. (One must use the phrase *white Americans* because equality of opportunity often has been denied to many people of color.) A white American of high intelligence might not become rich, but was likely to achieve at least a comfortable income. He or she would almost certainly receive a college education and would enter a social and economic class composed of others with similar ability. There were—and continue to be—exceptions, but the general rule became well established and its results became observable.

It was not simply a small elite that was removed from manual labor. Millions of Americans performed skilled work for which they were well paid. Their positions were won by ability. Most individuals of high IQ had traveled to a station where they worked and lived with other individuals of high IQ. They married within this station, as did their children. There was much less regression toward the mean than in the past. Equality of opportunity meant that people were socially and economically stratified by virtue of their intelligence.

The implications for our society are greater than those of any revolution that has ever occurred. What is happening now has never happened before, and its most ominous result could be the death of democracy.

★   ★   ★

The princes and generals who once ruled the West did not justify their sovereignty on the grounds of superior intelligence. Indeed, for them "intelligence" had quite a different meaning. An individual might be called "clever," but that was not necessarily a compliment; it connoted a form of shrewdness close to trickery. Some rulers were known as "wise"—a more favorable appellation—but the reference here was to judgment, not intellect. What was meant was a sort of articulated common sense.

Whatever word was used, it had nothing to do with the right to govern. That was determined by force. It was not necessary to state that "might made right"; it was an obvious truth. The winners of the battle ruled the rest. What was carved out by the sword was retained thereafter partially through the force of habit and custom: sovereignty was hereditary until some new power took it away. Of course, monarchs and peers whose station was derived from birth felt the need to justify the order that ensured their succession, and they did not claim that that justification was the capacity of their brains. Instead, they endorsed less vulnerable theories, chief among them the divine right of kings. It was the Lord's will that they should rule. The sovereign was carrying out his role in the ordained scheme of things. The aristocrats were able to justify their position, too. They saw the key as training, not capacity. They had been trained from birth in the arts of governance, which their hereditary privileges permitted them to exercise with relative disinterest. When a new class arose, moneyed but untitled, it explained its share of power in terms of property; those with the greatest stake in society would be most vigilant in its preservation. None of these rationales had anything to do with individual characteristics.

Approximately two centuries ago, however, things began to change. A new idea called democracy struck the tinder of revolution and, in an amazingly short time, became the accepted goal of the peoples of the West.

Democracy rests on the belief that all persons are created equal. This view of equality does not mean that all persons have the same ability, but rather that ability is randomly distributed. This notion is regarded as so obvious as to be beyond dispute. Equality is presented as an observable truth, held to be self-evident.

And it was. Everyone knew that the cobbler was more intelligent than the prince, or at least that some cobblers were more able than some princes. Even some princes realized that truth, but if they noticed that their tutors or their tailors had better minds than they, they did not see how that affected their role in society. That role was determined by God, custom, training, or the need for a stable order. There was no point to the fact that some people of low station had superior intelligence, just as there was no point to the fact that some people, of all ranks, were left-handed.

It is important to note what was new about democracy. It was not the observation that ability is randomly distributed. It was the attachment of political significance to that observation. The political significance attached to the fact that wisdom is widely scattered is that all people should be permitted to govern: the will of the majority should prevail.

Majority rule was the radical message of democracy. At first, it was a limited message, since the franchise was restricted to propertied males. Only a minority of the real populace could vote, but within that minority, the majority prevailed. The idea became fixed and was adhered to, while the definition of citizenry slowly expanded. Eventually, it became a true majority that had the power to sanction social change.

The idea was not merely that the majority must decide. By itself, that idea would have been only a variant of the old concern for social order, this time buttressed by consent. At the heart of the doctrine of majority rule was the express conviction that the majority was right. The majority *should* rule, because it knew best.

Yet sometimes it seemed that the majority was wrong. Certain decisions were discredited by subsequent events. When this occurred, the true majoritarian did not abandon his basic faith. There were explanations for the error. The people had not been given all the necessary facts; crafty leaders had betrayed them; the circumstance of crisis had precluded careful thought; the question had not been put properly. Despite or perhaps because of these excuses, the idea of majority rule was generally held to be consistent with the retention of broad powers by elected representatives. Those representatives had only to face the approval of the voters on a regular basis. When things went wrong, it was assumed that the representatives had been out of touch with the will of the majority. The best correction lay in their replacement.

Almost everyone used to believe this. It was the most basic assumption in political life. It was not merely the majority that believed in majority rule; the minority usually held with it, too—even that tiniest of minorities, the intellectual elite. Liberal intellectuals not only gave lip service to majoritarianism; their commitment to it was heartfelt, outspoken, and profound.

To some this was surprising. On the surface, it might have seemed strange that highly educated people—college professors, for example—should place their faith in the judgments of the many. But liberal intellectuals in the Western democracies had always been most acutely aware that they had something very important in common with the mass of people: powerlessness. They saw that real power had always been vested in the rich; it was the inheritors and managers of corporate and private wealth who were solidly in control. The only effective force that could counter this power was the will of the majority.

In America, many liberal intellectuals had the best possible reason for assuming that members of the working class would be their allies: the intellectuals themselves had just emerged from that class and still shared many of its values. They did not talk about The People in an aloof and abstract sense; they *knew* the people, or at least felt they did. Those people were their childhood friends, their relatives. Belief in the wisdom of The People was almost an article of faith.

That faith also included the advancement of racial minorities and the protection of civil liberties, but there was no inconsistency in this. A written constitution that gave absolute protection to certain minority rights, regardless of the popular mood, was really a corollary to the belief in majority rule.

Nowhere was that belief, that faith, as pronounced and fervent as in the United States. And this was true at least until the end of World War II. It was the theme of all those Frank Capra films. The Common Man was Capra's constant hero; his villains were the rich—owners of factories, of vast tracts of land, and very significantly, of newspapers. The quintessential Capra villain— the majoritarian's Antichrist—was the newspaper publisher in *Meet John Doe,* whose newspaper prevents the public from knowing the truth. The publisher disseminates slurs about John Doe, and the decent majority is thereby confused. When the hero tries to speak to the public directly—at a huge rally— the publisher's goons cut the microphone wires so that no one can hear the speech. The newspaper as antimajoritarian force is portrayed just as vividly in Capra's *Mr. Smith Goes to Washington,* in which a U.S. senator acts on the orders of a corrupt publisher and ignores the public will.

Both films were immensely popular in the 1930s; their descriptions of a society in which the majority was the defender of virtue and justice against the manipulations of the rich and privileged were consistent with the attitude of most liberal intellectuals.

But after World War II, this began to change. A new law was passed that may have altered American society more than any other piece of federal legislation in our history. It was known popularly as the GI Bill of Rights. The generous response of a grateful postwar public, this law provided tuition money to any returning veteran who was able to go to college. There were twelve million returning veterans, and an extraordinary number of them took advantage of this new law. Immediately, the percentage of Americans who attended college doubled, and shortly thereafter, it doubled again. There were millions of new students on the campuses, most of them from economic backgrounds that once would have precluded college attendance. Academics braced for the assault. Deans and professors consoled one another over an anticipated decline in standards, but the results astonished them. These new students were very good indeed. As a class, they were as good as the upper-income students, whose tuition was paid by their families. It was undeniably clear that general intelligence—or at least the ability to obtain good college grades—was very widely distributed throughout the American population, on all economic and social levels.

More significantly, higher education was no longer the privilege of the chosen few. Millions of Americans now saw it as their right; before long, it was regarded almost as a prerequisite to a decent job and income. Campuses were expanded and new colleges were built to accommodate the change in national expectations.

However, the principle established by this was not that all Americans have a right to a diploma, but, rather, that every person has the right to be educated to the best of his or her ability. The poor might be just as qualified for higher education as the rich; it was just a question of finding *which* poor were qualified. It became a matter of testing. Once the proper tests were devised and given to all children, the ablest could be identified and educated accordingly. Money was no longer an insurmountable barrier. Vast new scholarship programs supplanted the GI Bill. Suddenly, the only barrier to most (white) Americans who wanted to continue their schooling was their own ability. A previous generation had jokingly asked, "If he's so smart, why isn't he rich?" The postwar generation was more inclined to see it this way: "If he's so smart, why isn't he educated?" There were, of course, obvious examples of brilliant achievers—business executives, inventors, statesmen, even a president—who had not attended college. But they were older and they had been raised in a different era.

The testing programs worked very well. The brightest boys and girls, no matter what their background, swarmed to the campuses, there to win their diplomas and find their careers. It should be noted that *brighter* and *more intelligent* are used here for convenience only, as synonyms for "having higher IQs," even though it is understood that IQ tests probably measure only some aspects of intelligence, such as verbal skills, and may contain a cultural bias that unfairly penalizes those from deprived backgrounds. The point is not that the tests are accurate—they are not—but that they are mistakenly *believed* to be accurate and are therefore self-fulfilling. *Something* is being tested, and our society wrongly assumes that that something is general intelligence. The possession of that something, many people are told, makes them superior to others. That something is also rewarded by society. And that something *seems* to be heritable, though it may be transmitted in significant part through environmental factors.

So young people with higher IQs were first identified and then segregated on campuses during the same years in which many of them chose their marriage partners. It was understandable that proximity would affect choice. For the first time in the history of this planet, stratification by IQ was almost ensured. The boy with an IQ of 137 married the girl with an IQ of 141. Their children might not have IQs as high as those of either parent—because of the natural tendency toward the mean—but their intelligence would almost certainly be higher than the average. These children are members of the new class, too, educated as highly as their parents and likely to mate with others of similar background. The new class is therefore self-perpetuating, and it seems to be permanent.

It is self-segregated as well—particularly by association. Once its members are off the campuses, they usually work and live only with one another. When there is contact with others, the outsiders are usually in subservient roles—janitors, domestic help, gas station attendants, taxi drivers. The greater number of outsiders—those who punch time clocks in factories, for instance—are never seen at all. It is impossible to exaggerate how insular this new class has become. Its members talk only to one another. They have little awareness of what the rest of the country is like.

★   ★   ★

The emergent class of those who believe themselves to be measurably brighter than everyone else can be known as the New Elite. A novelty in human experience, it is (except for the Chinese Mandarins) the first powerful social class in history whose membership is defined by measurable intelligence. Everyone not in this class can be referred to—in terms of how the New Elite sees them—as the Left Behinds.

These terms are not near synonyms for older labels. The New Elite and the Left Behinds are not necessarily synonymous with other pairs in confrontation: liberals and conservatives, Democrats and Republicans, upper-middle class and lower-middle class. Correlations may be made, but they are misleading and quick to change. One need not have attended college to be a member of the New Elite; a privileged dropout qualifies. A professor of philosophy at Princeton could easily be one of the Left Behinds if his or her basic identity is with a traditional social or economic or ethnic group. *The deciding point in every case is how individuals see themselves.* If an individual has strong roots in a social class or religion, in the values of an urban neighborhood or the farmland or country club life, then the fact that one's intelligence has once been measured as above the average may not be a critical point in self-identity or allegiance. But if such roots are absent, or if they have been rejected, one may assume a self-identity as an individual of measured superiority and find a class allegiance with other individuals of similar measurement. There is no admissions committee for either the New Elite or the Left Behinds. Each person is automatically a member of the class to which he assumes he belongs.

You can't be a member of the New Elite unless you see yourself primarily as intelligent rather than as something else. We all tend to think that society could benefit from the counsel of people like ourselves. Those who, when they say "ourselves," mean those with the highest measurable intelligence are members of the New Elite. Those who, when they say "ourselves," mean anything else—other businessmen or scientists or artists or women or Catholics or liberals or conservatives or Texans or Frenchmen or laborers or Mayflower descendants or farmers or dukes or millionaires or "We the People"—are members of the Left Behinds. Rejection of roots is a prerequisite for membership in the New Elite; adherence to roots (or class or caste or faith) is the primary barrier to such membership.

Sometimes one can tell the New Elite from the Left Behinds by what they do for a living. Care is required, however; occupation alone is not an infallible guide. And it's not simply a question of how much intelligence is required to perform a certain job. What really counts is whether the job is based on certain testable skills. Doctors, lawyers, architects, academicians, scientists, certain types of executives, many levels of government bureaucrats, some journalists, and others who deal in verbal skills have all met the threshold test for the New Elite. But it must be remembered that it's only a *threshold* test; any members of those professions may be Left Behinds—if that's how they see themselves.

People whose work does not require professional, verbal, or technocratic skills are probably Left Behinds. This includes most small businessmen, retailers, manufacturers, manual and clerical workers, and salespeople. In a large corporation, the top executives and the assembly line workers are typically Left Behinds, while the upper–middle ranks—analysts, lawyers, researchers—belong to the New Elite.

The New Elite ranking of job status is based on how removed a person's work is from ratification by the public. Those whose success or failure is judged solely by their professional peers are likely to be part of the New Elite. Those whose success depends in part on public approval are Left Behinds. Salesmen are an obvious example, and so are most businessmen. Using the public ratification test, the most Left Behind occupation of all should be holding elective office—or at least this used to be the case.

The New Elite feels that it's good to have money, but not too much. It knows that really great wealth is seldom the salaried reward for testable technical and verbal skills. The nuclear physicist makes much less money than the owner of a uranium mine. Since great wealth suggests an occupation divorced from testable skills, the New Elite cultivates a lifestyle that connotes modest prosperity, not opulence. A Volvo wins more points than a Mercedes; a mink coat at a faculty party is a social disaster. One sometimes hears the new class referred to as the "wine and brie set." This taunt is not without significance; it helps locate its target on the economic scale: wine and brie are not beer and pretzels, but neither are they champagne and caviar.

The real significance of the New Elite is political. Its members are the managers of society—teachers, commentators, planners, officials, and executives—the articulators of thoughts and standards. In a society that rewards ability, the New Elite possesses influence far out of proportion to its numbers.

But it does not have political control. It has political power, certainly, but not political dominance. Democracy is based on majority rule, and the New Elite does not constitute a majority. To be sure, it is a large class and is growing while other classes are shrinking, but it's still a long, long way from 50 percent and knows that it's unlikely ever to enjoy majority strength.

At first, this was not a problem. So long as many recent members of the New Elite shared some background and values with the Left Behinds, they shared the same political goals, too. Majorities were formed with members of both classes. But as time went on, the values changed within the New Elite. Now most of its members are not the children of the working class but the children of the New Elite.

Those who are economically comfortable see things differently from those who are not. They want different things. For example, the well-off might be more concerned with halting inflation than with an increase in the minimum wage. Furthermore, the affluent can afford to be concerned about things other than economic survival and to some extent can view the social issues of the day with relative disregard for their economic consequences. This permits them to be, or at least to feel that they are, freer in their thinking, more dispassionate and just.

The first great issue to split the two classes was the civil rights movement. The New Elite endorsed it, and the Left Behinds did not. More precisely, the New Elite was for much swifter and more comprehensive change. This was perfectly understandable, for nothing is more consistent with the New Elite experience than that individuals should be judged by their abilities as individuals rather than as members of a social class—or race. Many Left Behinds felt threatened by the move toward racial equality because they regarded their status and, in some cases, their jobs as protected by their color. Although not all New Elitists supported the civil rights movement, and not all Left Behinds opposed it, the class dichotomy was clear. With public consciousness raised, the civil rights movement made considerable progress, but not nearly so much or so quickly as its advocates desired.

The second great issue was the war in Vietnam. Here, too, the new class lines were imperfectly drawn. Generally, the New Elite opposed the war earlier than the Left Behinds and was far more fervent in its opposition.

These two issues had a profound impact on the political perceptions of the New Elite. To some extent, its ideology had prevailed, but its efforts had also been frustrated, delayed, and even, in particular skirmishes, defeated. The New Elite felt, correctly, that with regard to both issues it had been right, although it had faced what seemed at times to be not only opposition but opposition by the majority.

Both the civil rights movement and the peace movement had made efforts to win over the majority. Bright and principled young students had traveled to the South on behalf of racial justice and had rung doorbells in New Hampshire for Eugene McCarthy's presidential campaign. For the first time in many years, the New Elite was coming face-to-face with the Left Behinds. The meeting was not propitious. The Dartmouth junior rang doorbells, but he did not always like the people who came to open the door. They were usually not at all like the people to whom he was accustomed. They did not always share his point of view. And, as often happens when others don't agree with us, he thought they were stupid. Everything in his experience supported this conclusion. Their speech did not conform to the rules of grammar. If they read books and magazines, they were the wrong ones. Their taste was awful. They had pink plastic flamingos on their lawns and huge chrome gas eaters in their driveways. They were selfish, not altruistic; closed, not open; instinctive, not rational. They were stupid.

And, should anyone doubt that finding, there was always the obvious question: If they were so smart, how come they weren't educated? Before long, a corollary question formed in the minds of the New Elite: Why should one of *their* votes count the same as one of ours? It now was doubtful that the New Elite would endorse the values of a Frank Capra film. The newspaper publisher had become its class ally and the common man something of a villain.

★   ★   ★

For the first time in the Western democratic tradition, many educated liberals no longer instinctively believe in majority rule. Subconsciously, they have begun to reject the most basic tenet of all. They no longer believe that all men are created equal. That was merely a way of saying that ability was randomly scattered throughout all levels of society, and they can see this is no longer true of measured intelligence. But so inbred in our culture is the conviction that the majority is right that the new disbelief has remained beneath the surface of awareness. It has permeated attitude but not yet conscious thought.

The members of the New Elite are engaged in doublethink. They give lip service to the majoritarian principle and even invoke it with passion on those occasions when their side outnumbers the opposition. While some believe that majoritarianism is right, in their actions they are antimajoritarian. Politically, their ceaseless strategy is inconsistent with their professed thought.

How can one profess to believe in majority rule and yet seek to subvert its results? The New Elite has developed a number of strategies for this purpose, and their use is growing. These strategies must be subtle enough to allow an expressed belief in what they seek to undermine and yet permit those who employ them to ignore this basic contradiction.

The easiest of these strategies is to identify a majority group and then claim to be speaking on behalf of all its members. A consumer advocate can claim to be speaking on behalf of all consumers, which is to say everybody. An activist can oppose a new construction project in the name of all who live near the site. Never mind that the spokesperson has neglected to obtain the consent of those he or she "represents," and never mind that the majority in question exists only with regard to a specific characteristic or interest, its members sharing no consensus beyond that. But, of course, people *do* mind, which limits the effectiveness of this tactic. It is a tactic inconsistent with the majoritarian tradition in two basic regards. First, majority rule means *consenting* majority rule; second, a true majority is an accumulation of individuals. Such groups have no political significance until their members express themselves as individuals. If the members of a group do agree with one another, then they will prevail—as a totality of individual expression. It is ironic that the New Elite, which sprang from the measurement and reward of individual ability, should seek to deny the role of the individual and instead find its focus in the arbitrary constructs of convenient groupings.

Another tactic is the growing reliance on the doctrine of negative consent. Here, a self-appointed spokesperson claims to be the democratically elected representative of a special-interest group whose members are supposed to have given their consent when, in fact, they have not. It works like this. The members of a group, such as all students on one campus, are informed that some individuals will be representing their interests. If a student does not want to be so represented, he or she must vote disapproval at a designated time and place. Unless this is done, it is assumed that the student has consented to the representation. This tactic is widely employed within the Public Interest Research Groups founded by the Nader organization on many campuses. Since many students either don't know about the negative option or neglect to exercise it, the resulting "representation" is extensive. Such negative consent lacks the element of true volition. It is similar to the marketing technique employed by some book clubs: anyone who doesn't indicate by a certain date that the monthly selection is *not* desired will be billed for it. (Such contracts have been attacked by Nader as unfair to consumers.)

Then there is the tactic of the Most Convenient Majority. (It can also be called the Doctrine of the Variable Whole.) This tactic *does* rely on the consent of a true majority, but a very small one. Suppose a new housing project is proposed for a large city and a majority of the few hundred residents near the project site oppose any new construction. The project is defeated. Perhaps several million citizens of the greater metropolitan area favored the project and would have benefited from it. No matter. Opponents can—and do— claim that a majority, however limited in number, sanctions their cause.

None of the methods described here has been used directly in the political process. So far, their employment has been limited to large interest groups other than political parties. The goal has been to achieve spokesperson status in representing those groups and to use that status to bring pressure on elected officials. When a local legislator is told that the lobbyist calling on him represents one million consumers or one hundred thousand students, he may believe those claims. It could make all the difference in determining his vote.

But real power goes far beyond lobbying. Real power is transferred in elections. From the New Elite point of view, this arrangement has a tragic flaw. In general elections, the candidate with the most votes wins. While this might seem an insurmountable barrier, the New Elite has found a way around it. Elections may be decided by the people, but the candidates are chosen by political parties. If the New Elite can gain control of one, or both, of the political parties, it can choose the candidate itself.

This is to be accomplished by changing the rules. The central tactic is to achieve political party rules that minimize majority participation, thereby permitting a small faction to gain control of the whole. This process is well under way; it helps explain our presidential campaigns for at least the past three decades.

The greatest restriction on majority representation has come from the use of various formulas to apportion delegate votes. These formulas originally were meant to avoid the old practice of winner take all and to give each candidate a fair share of delegates. However, in the hands of the New Elite, they serve another purpose, by becoming so complicated and difficult that only graduate students can understand them.

The complexity of these rules poses the greatest threat to majoritarianism. There are several varieties of proportional voting, some very complicated and difficult at first to understand. They may not have been designed to be confusing, but that is their effect. The significant fact is that many of the rule changes are more confusing to some voters than to others; that is, they are much more of a problem for the Left Behinds than they are for the New Elite. Well-educated people may not be intimidated by lengthy voting instructions, but others may be so dismayed that they cease to participate in the process. The loss of these participants represents a critical and growing threat to our political system.

Majority rule means not just the number of votes that it takes to prevail, but also the absence of restrictions on the right to vote. In internal party contests, the New Elite has sponsored rules and voting procedures so complex and time-consuming that they restrict the average person's role in party affairs. Senior citizens sit bewildered at precinct caucuses while the subtlest nuances of the Hare system are slowly intoned in redundant detail. A post office clerk leaves the meeting at midnight because the first ballot of the evening has not yet been taken and she must report to work by seven the next morning. Those who do stick it out may well decide never to return. Their right to participate has been effectively discouraged. Labyrinthine rules and lengthy meetings are the poll tax that the New Elite has been imposing on everyone else.

The damage to the caucus system at the hands of the New Elite is one reason for the relatively recent increase in the number of primary elections. Many states whose political parties operated under the caucus system have switched over to primaries. This is particularly regrettable, because the caucus system— when properly conducted—is clearly compatible with majoritarian democracy. Arguably, it is better in this regard than the primary. Now, candidates of both parties are selected in primaries involving fewer and fewer voters.

Despite the assaults against it, rule by the majority is still safeguarded by most of our political institutions. Though partially eroded within the political parties, it remains the proclaimed and intrinsic norm of our society. Members of the New Elite continue to see their most cherished hopes and beliefs fail to proceed, because they lack majority support. All their lives they have been accustomed to swift gratification of their wants, and they are impatient now at the slowness of their efforts to gain political control. Reinforced by one another that their views are right, increasingly convinced that they will not become a numerical majority, they are beginning to openly attack not merely the procedures but the very idea of majority rule.

Their attack is, for the most part, indirect. Perhaps even now they do not recognize the implications. On a variety of fronts, however, they advocate positions that are incompatible with the assumption that the majority should prevail.

One of these positions has to do with moral right. The New Elite claims moral superiority in order to bypass the need for obtaining majority support. It holds that a view should prevail if the New Elite believes it to be morally superior to an opposing view, regardless of the number of people who support either side of the issue. A New Elitist thinks and says that "I and my friends should have our way on this matter because we are morally right. It does not matter that the majority opposes us, because the majority is morally wrong. Moral right should prevail over numerical superiority."

This view does have some roots in our democratic tradition—roots, but not parallels. It was always understood that the decision of the majority might offend the consciences of some in the minority, and this possibility was respected. The majoritarian idea does not foreclose the role of private conscience. There is an honored place not only for moral dissent but also for moral resistance, as there is a place for civil disobedience. But the idea has always been that moral resistance should be used to instruct the majority, not supplant it.

It is here that New Elitists are breaking with tradition. Whether deliberately or through ignorance, they miss the point made by the advocates of civil disobedience. Thoreau did not seek to prevail but to resist. He understood that there were penalties attached to his dissent and that the payment of those penalties was an intrinsic part of dissent. It was in this fashion that one could honor personal conviction regardless of what the majority felt.

But New Elitists read the classic texts more narrowly; for them it is all Walden Pond and no Concord Jail. When their views are opposed by the majority, they seldom claim the right to carry out those views regardless of legal sanction. Nor do they often urge disobedience as a tool to change the majority's view. That would be to concede that the final decision is up to the majority. Instead, they claim that the majority doesn't matter, that the minority view should be accepted at once and by all because of its inherent moral superiority.

The use of moral argument has been reinforced by recent history. The New Elite *was* morally right with regard to racial equality and the war in Vietnam. In both areas, it saw itself outnumbered, and in both it eventually won some success because the majority was persuaded of the merits of each cause. The moral argument was *accepted* by the majority. One might well conclude that the experience was an affirmation of democratic procedures.

But the New Elite saw it as an affirmation of moral protest. It applauded the tactic and not its response. The New Elite began to invoke a moral tactic in areas where its application was less appropriate than it was in issues such as war and race. The word *immoral* is now used by New Elitists as a simple synonym for *wrong*. Any view not in agreement with the New Elite becomes immoral. Graduate student delegates to a political convention in the Midwest denounce the use of pay toilets as immoral, and their peers applaud the description. It is no longer a question of converting the majority. The use of the word *immoral* is not intended to win arguments but to preclude them. It is a magic formula whose utterance is supposed to bring automatic support.

The word *immoral* has been debased through overuse, hence a priceless resource in the battle for liberal progress has been lost. It is not possible to mobilize the citizenry against political torture in foreign prisons with the same vocabulary that is used to denounce SUVs.

★   ★   ★

Everywhere in America today, there is an assault on the idea that the people can determine their own policies. That assault has had its effect on every institution in our society and on every branch of government. It explains why so much decision making has been plucked from the legislative branch and dropped on the federal courts. The rejection of the principle of judicial self-restraint coincided with the postwar rise of the influence of the New Elite. The emergent class did not share Justice Felix Frankfurter's faith in the wisdom of the majority. Its members were far more disposed to see weighty issues resolved by lifetime judges, who were gifted people like themselves. So courts today have mandated in exquisite detail schemes that deserve the insights and priorities of representative legislation.

There are still other tactics for avoiding majority rule. There is the growth of support for "pluralism," the autonomous rule of specific constituencies. There is the effort to appropriate to one's cause all those votes that were never cast: "The 60 percent of the voters who stayed home were really supporting me."

But the fact that the New Elite is grasping for power on every front doesn't mean it has a specific platform it wishes to impose. Aside from a vague desire to restrict the growth of society, to limit wealth and thereby weaken the link between wealth and status, it has no program, no ideology, no agenda. The ultimate political objective of the New Elite is not so much concerned with *what* government does as with *who* does the governing. The New Elite devoutly feels that what is best for society is that society be governed by the New Elite.

In politics, what matters to the New Elite is not so much what a candidate is *for* as who he or she *is*. The critical thing is to find out whether the person is a New Elitist. Intelligence, education, and views on the issues are not the only qualifications necessary to win support; these merely provide the threshold. What really matters is whether the candidate thinks that human experience has a bearing on human problems. The New Elite refuses to balance reason with experience. It enshrines the former and rejects the latter.

In the New Elite's determination of whom to support, details about the personal life of a candidate are very important. If he worships regularly at the same neighborhood church that his parents and grandparents attended, he is likely to be in thrall to tradition. Lifestyle and appearance are very useful guides in determining who really belongs to the New Elite, and positions on the issues are almost irrelevant.

Politically, the New Elite is concerned with style over substance. The way to win over many of the best-educated voters is by emphasizing image, not issues. The Left Behinds, particularly the working class, are more likely to decide among candidates on the basis of the specific programs that they advocate, especially with regard to economic issues. But the Left Behinds, too, are increasingly concerned with image, desperately searching for candidates with the same roots, experience, and values that they themselves have known.

It is possible for a candidate to appeal simultaneously to both groups. John F. Kennedy is the classic case. Many Left Behinds supported him because they could identify with his roots—his religion, the closeness of his family, his pride in his immigrant forebears. They liked the fact that he listened to Kenny O'Donnell. The New Elite admired his style. They heard the accent of Harvard, not Boston. They liked his clothes and his wit, the quotes from Aeschylus, the cello concert in the East Room. They liked the fact that he listened to Arthur Schlesinger Jr.

Thus, Kennedy could make the supposed missile gap with the Soviet Union the central thrust of his campaign without sacrificing the votes, or enthusiasm, of the New Elite—most of whose members were supporting reductions in defense spending. And he could become a champion of the civil rights movement without alienating a large working-class following, whose own views on race were often narrow. He proved that what one says he's in favor of counts for much less than who he seems to be.

Sometimes even the same phrase, if carefully crafted, could please both audiences. The most popular line of Kennedy's inaugural address was "Ask not what your country can do for you, but what you can do for your country." Each side heard these words differently. For the Left Behinds, Kennedy was evoking the most traditional values: patriotism, discipline, sacrifice for the common welfare. For the New Elite, Kennedy was saying that the nation had no obligation to provide for the welfare of all its citizens; it had, in fact, a claim on their service for that which government itself determined was a proper cause of action. What John Kennedy did is not possible today; a candidate can no longer placate both camps and attract a true majority. Such has been the impact of the New Elite on our political life.

All the strange new activity of the decades since Kennedy has shown how the efforts of the New Elite could deny the democratic process. The vilification of political parties; the ascendancy of image over issues; the disrespect for law (which is a codification of majority will); the substitution of stridency for debate, of rallies for elections, and of rigidity for compromise; the shifting of power from Congress to the courts; the growth of interest groups that bypass and disdain the political process; the self-appointment of spokespersons; the denigration and corruption of popular culture; the rejection of traditional values; the enthronement of the "expert"; the enactment of rules that limit political participation in the name of extending it—all these things are rooted in the new belief that the majority does not, cannot, know what's best, that there exists a group that is measurably superior to everybody else, and that no statute or habit or procedure must be allowed to stand between that group and dominance.

Our society has scarcely become aware of the nature of the threat against it. That awareness should bring both the will and the strength to respond, because the New Elite is wrong in its perception of democracy. The majority *should* prevail. This is as true today as it was before the introduction of the Stanford–Binet Test. It will always be true. It is true because the capacity to make broad political choices is not related to measurable intelligence. This was assumed by those who wrote "all men are created equal." If that phrase had meant that measurable intelligence is randomly scattered throughout the population, then it would indeed no longer be true. But it did not. It meant that *ability* is widely scattered, specifically the ability to make political judgments. And that is as true now as always. The eternal truth is that political wisdom is not an attribute of intelligence or education or class or gender or race. It is the response to experience. In terms of the capacity to make political choices, the most significant response to human experience is the view one comes to hold of human nature. No one person or group has the right to define what human nature is. Each view is burdened by personal experience. We cannot prove, by logic or calculation, just whose version is correct. Only the majority knows, because only the majority view approaches the aggregate of human experience. We must mine the whole vein. We must ask everyone's opinion and let the majority prevail.

THREE

Who They Are

Charlene's parents were not exactly poor. They owned their own home in Allentown, Pennsylvania—a modest but very well-maintained house. There was always enough to eat and the children did not lack for clothing. Money was somehow found for birthday presents, holiday parties, and family outings at a nearby lake.

But there is not much joy in Charlene's recollection of her past, of which she remembers a great deal. She remembers having to wear her older sister's clothes, which though clean and unpatched were somewhat out of style. She remembers furniture that was nondescript, heavy, and cheap. She remembers that there were no magazines in her house and very few books. She remembers being rather embarrassed, almost ashamed, when friends saw her neighborhood, her home, her family. None of her grandparents was born in this country, and neither of her parents attended college. Charlene was distressed by the way her father spoke and annoyed by the narrowness of her mother's interests.

Charlene attended the public school nearest her home. It did not take long for her teachers to realize that she was a very gifted student. She received high grades and constant praise and eventually was encouraged to skip a grade; though younger than her new classmates, she continued to do superior work. The sciences and mathematics were her particular strengths.

By the tenth grade, Charlene discovered what she had had no opportunity to know at home: the beauty of classical music. She learned to play the violin. She also managed to build a large record collection, which she kept in her room.

Charlene graduated as the salutatorian of her high school class and received a science scholarship to Temple University in Philadelphia. Even with the scholarship, the costs of attending college away from home were high, so Charlene found a part-time job, and her parents did what they could to help out.

College opened up a whole new world to Charlene. Despite the fifteen hours a week she spent clerking at a drugstore, she was able to maintain outstanding grades. She found the time to make new friends and was delighted to discover others who shared her interests. Her new friends seemed far more stimulating than those she had left behind, and she felt proud to be accepted by them as an equal. There were so many things to do: concerts and lectures and long talks about them later. Charlene joined the Vivaldi Club and also learned to play tennis.

After receiving her B.A. (magna cum laude), Charlene moved on to graduate school at Cornell; she had decided to pursue a career in microbiology. She worked very hard and did extremely well, and by the time she had her master's degree, Charlene was able to devote herself to her doctorate without the distraction of outside work; increased scholarships and a major federal grant covered all her financial needs.

Charlene married a fellow graduate student, a physicist from New York. After receiving their Ph.D.s, they moved to Seattle, where she became a teaching assistant at the University of Washington and her husband found a research position with an aerospace company.

Their life together is very pleasant. The house they bought (before the real-estate boom) is perfectly suited to their zest for restoration. Their neighbors are mostly young professionals. On one side lives the assistant city budget director and his wife, a law student; on the other lives a systems analyst. The houses are old, but the occupants are new. Few of them were born in Seattle and most, like Charlene and her husband, are very recent arrivals. They have their newness in common; initially, it was the basis for their friendships. There is no need for them to go elsewhere for companionship. The social life of the neighborhood is largely self-contained.

Very few are rich, but almost all are better off than their parents were. Many households have two professional incomes. They can afford new furniture—not, perhaps, the opulent selections of the decorator magazines, but surely good enough. They enjoy having dinner in one another's homes; there is candlelight and wine and much sharing of recipes for, say, ratatouille or an exotic curry. While they like to eat in restaurants occasionally, they scorn the most expensive of these as "tourist traps" and hunt with competitive zeal for some "authentic" fare—Syrian, Greek, Thai, or Japanese. Their quest runs precisely contrary to Chicago columnist Mike Royko's advice to "stick to restaurants of an ethnic group large enough to have two aldermen." Their taste in clothing favors authenticity, too; some resemble prairie gentry of the nine-teenth century. And there is enough disposable income to indulge a flowering of interests: foreign films, local crafts, concerts, travel.

Sometimes, when Charlene looks at her young son, Josh, she can't help comparing his upbringing with her own. She is proud of the differences but also a little resentful. It isn't so much the material things—they are raising Josh not to think in such terms—as a question of atmosphere. His childhood seems so much more serene than hers. There is no worry about money and there is unlimited opportunity. The future is secure.

Charlene does not want anything in her life to change. She is very con-tent with things as they are for her and her family. She knows that things will get even better with the passing of years, that there will be a gradual increase in the household income, as both professionals increase their seniority. She wants nothing to disrupt her good life and her plans for Josh's future. She does not want large outside forces to alter in any way her family's steady destiny. She wants to be left alone.

Charlene feels that she has earned her better way of life, that she has risen to her natural level, to the place where she belongs. The same is true of her husband and many of their friends, some of whom left behind backgrounds that they, too, regard with the same embarrassment as she does her own. She is grateful to have escaped a world that was devoid of verve or culture, in which no one had heard of Bach or Bartók, coquilles or quiches, Sondheim or Son-tag, feta or PETA, Bilbo or Bilbao.

She is grateful, but to whom? To what? What was it that had wafted her to such improved circumstances? It must have been her own ability, which en-lightened people had recognized and rewarded. The same is true for her friends. They have achieved what they deserve.

Gratitude breeds loyalty. How can Charlene feel loyalty to values and roots she has rejected? How can she avoid a strong allegiance to the new way of life that she has won with her own mind? And if her friends and neighbors hold a particular point of view, how can she doubt the superiority of that view since their own superiority is evidenced by what they have achieved?

Charlene is a member of the New Elite and has much in common with other members of her class. She shares with them not only certain taste in clothes and books and films, but also the same attitude. They reject the past. They disdain tradition. They believe in themselves. Like everyone else, their view of society, based on their own experience, reflects their own interests.

★　★　★

Edward is very affluent, and this sets him apart from many other Left Behinds. He is quite intelligent, too; his IQ is actually higher than Charlene's. Yet he could never be a member of the New Elite, and it is instructive to see why.

Edward grew up in Mankato, Minnesota, then a prosperous town of thirty thousand. His father—and *his* father before him—was a partner in the town's leading law firm. It represented the largest local bank, two of the three biggest businesses in the area, and more than its share of wealthy farmers. Edward's father was one of the leading citizens in Mankato. He served on many boards, both business and civic, and he had been president of the local country club. Everyone knew who he was.

Edward grew up very much aware of his family's place in the scheme of things. Each day brought new reminders of who he was. The mention of his surname produced a knowing look and smiles. He saw respect in the eyes of the parents of his friends. His teachers were very friendly.

Mankato is not that large a town. Many families have been there for several generations. Everyone seems to know everyone else. There is no private secular school in the town, so the sons and daughters of the rich and poor are educated together. This commingling did not detract from Edward's sense of his family's place; it strengthened it. He felt himself part of a community and knew very well his own role in it.

Edward had a very happy youth. His easy manner and athletic skill ensured his popularity. He was bright, and his parents had instilled in him the habit of diligence. Despite playing football and tennis and being captain of the school golf team, he was able to finish near the top of his high school class. He had no trouble being accepted by Dartmouth, which his father had attended before him.

Edward's college years were a very pleasant extension of the life he had always known. Many of his classmates were from backgrounds similar to his. There were sports and girls and modest academic success. His fraternity was one of the best.

It never seriously occurred to Edward to seek his fortune outside of Mankato. He considered himself part of a very acceptable tradition. After graduation (cum laude) he enrolled in the University of Minnesota law school. His father had gone there, too, and it was supposedly very helpful to study law along with so many other future colleagues in the state bar.

Edward worked much harder in law school than he had in college, and at the end of his first year was asked to join the Law Review. His success was motivated by pride, not necessity. Regardless of where he finished in his class, a desk would be waiting for him in the family firm. He regarded this as an obligation to do well.

In the summer following his second year of law school, Edward married a young woman from Mankato whom he had known all his life. She had been at Smith, and he had dated her exclusively since his junior year. Her father owned a processing plant, and their parents were good friends.

The practice of law is the same in Mankato as anywhere else, except that Edward is able to walk home for lunch. He works very hard, with commendable results, but there is time for golf and active membership in the chamber of commerce and the church, and for fundraising for the local congressman. He helped lead the campaign to fund some sculpture for the town plaza.

Edward's home is near his parents', of which it is a smaller, newer version. Ostentation is avoided in their set, but Edward's wife has considerable flair and the leisure to indulge it. Theirs is a very comfortable life: dinners at the club and frequent trips to Minneapolis to see old friends and attend plays. They stay at home more often now that they have a son, Edward Jr.

It is impossible to think of Edward as a member of the New Elite, because it is impossible that he would think of himself as a member. That's the whole point. It's a matter of self-selection. Edward knows that he is intelligent, of course. That has been verified by tests and grades and in the competitive practice of law. Yet this has very little to do with the way he sees himself. Privately, he may harbor feelings of superiority, but these are quite divorced from any IQ scores. Other factors played major roles in shaping his strong sense of identity. He acknowledges his own ability but certainly doesn't see himself as a member of a class based on academic achievement. Instead, he sees himself as a local aristocrat, one whose family has always been among those who ran the town. He views himself also as a lawyer, as the literal heir to the standards of a profession. He sees himself as a Dartmouth man. He sees himself as a patriot. He sees himself as a golfer. If he had done less well in school—or if he'd done even better—his life and his values would not have been significantly altered. He feels he owes his comfortable status in life not so much to his measurable intelligence as to other things: a social order, an economic system, a society that rewards certain traits as well as testable skills. He is grateful to the traditional scheme of things.

★   ★   ★

The examples of Charlene and Edward were chosen to illustrate certain characteristics. Neither should be considered a prototype. It is not necessary to be as well educated as Charlene to be a member of the New Elite; many of its members have undistinguished and limited academic records. But if they hold jobs that require verbal or technical skills, and if they identify principally with similar types, then their class membership could be well established— even if their real intelligence is not. Edward is atypical of the Left Behinds because of his income and education, but he does represent the loyalty to roots and tradition that qualifies him for classification as a Left Behind—or, rather, that disqualifies him for the New Elite.

The point of the examples is this: membership in the New Elite is not determined so much by either IQ or education as it is by the rejection of traditional values. Most important, it is a matter of self-identification, a matter of self-inclusion in a class. If one's primary identity is with the new class of educated professionals, and if one shares its values (which are based on a rejection of traditional values), then one is a member of the New Elite.

In a sense, IQ is not very important at all. *Class identity and loyalty are what really matter.* The significance of measured intelligence is that it propels many into the class in the first place and serves to justify the class self-image and demands later on.

You don't have to be very bright to hold many of the jobs that lead to the rather uniform income range and lifestyle of the New Elite. In this sense, Charlene is an imperfect example because she has achieved real academic distinction and is employed as a scholar. Most members of the New Elite fall far short of her ability or attainments. A researcher for a state legislature, a public information officer of a corporation, a wide range of administrators, planners, copywriters, counselors, consultants, analysts, technicians, and hundreds of thousands of workers at middle-level jobs and of middling ability are members of the New Elite, too. Many of them are not remarkably gifted, cultivated, or exceptional, but they tend to have at least a college education and ostensible skills sufficient to hold down a vast and increasing number of jobs in a society where blue-collar workers are now a minority. They do not work with their hands. Their jobs, many of them routine, are often (but not always) more remunerative than physical labor. While they do not achieve huge rewards and they are seldom rich, their incomes permit comforts and attitudes sufficient to ensure a standard of living distinct from that of the traditional labor force.

This standard of living is pleasant enough to foster a sense of achievement and well-being. To many members of the New Elite, it represents an improvement over the environment in which they were raised and it allows them to think of themselves as members of a somewhat privileged class. It is enough to separate themselves (in their own view) from the great mass of people whom they feel they've left behind.

No matter how mediocre their talent or mundane their jobs, their sense of superiority is supported because they receive somewhat more money and status than many others. Because our society rewards their testable skills, they in time value their own skills even more highly. They identify with others of similar skills and jobs and rewards. A sense of class identity emerges. The first step is taken.

The emphasis on intelligence comes later—after the class allegiance has been formed, at which time it becomes almost essential. Intelligence is used to distinguish the New Elite from both ordinary workers who make nearly as much money and businessmen who make much more. It is used to confer particular status on a group that can never reach the highest income brackets. Those whose primary identity is with this new class quite naturally place great store on the value of measured intelligence—supposedly the key to their improved way of life. By emphasizing its origins, the New Elite defines itself as unique and seeks credibility for its insistence on a special role.

The formation of a large class of educated professionals was not possible until very recently. Several preconditions had to be met: an industrial society so far advanced that its economy could justify a major allocation of resources to management, research, and explication; many new jobs that could be filled not merely by members of a preexistent economic or social elite but by those to whom this new employment represented an improved standard of living with which they would want to identify, rather than seeing it as the extension of a previous caste; a social arrangement that identified the testable skills of its citizens and made it inevitable that most of those with certain skills would identify with—and marry—one another; a clustering, a segregation, of these skilled workers by neighborhood, by employment, by lifestyle, and above all, by family unit. Finally, there had to be the sense—necessary to the formation of any class—that what these people had in common could be handed down to their succeeding generations.

All of these conditions have been met, and a new class has been formed. Its members number in the millions. However, they do not include everyone with the requisite testable ability. While David Rockefeller has a Ph.D. in economics, one can surmise that his class identity is likely with an old financial elite. A devoutly Orthodox Jewish physicist may identify so strongly with his coreligionists that his sense of identity is unrelated to his profession. A doctor who is the son of a farmer may continue to think of himself in terms of his rural roots. The very brightest people in society—the most extraordinarily creative in their fields—may think of themselves as so superior to their coworkers that no sense of class can possibly occur to them.

Almost everyone sees the world in terms of Us and Them. Accordingly, Albert Einstein could not have been a member of the New Elite, for despite his remarkable intellectual gifts, he seems to have regarded his fellow humans as Us. Neither his writings nor his manner suggest that he saw himself as a member of any class, though he had a strong sense of identity with other scientists and fellow Jews. There is no evidence that he saw his genius at physics as testament to a right to determine social policy for others.

Pablo Picasso was not a member of the New Elite. He saw himself as an artist, and surely the question of IQ was irrelevant to what he felt himself to be. He was Picasso, and that was enough.

Henry Kissinger is not a member of the New Elite, though his academic credentials are exemplary. In his world, success is certified by power, not grades. His celebrated ego pertains to himself and not to any class.

Alexander the Great and Frederick the Great and William Pitt and Talleyrand and Bismarck and Disraeli might have considered themselves superior in ability to their contemporaries and more deserving than anyone else to govern human lives. But each saw *himself* this way. None saw a distinct class of the intellectually able to whom the reins of government belonged by right. Indeed, these rulers did feel some class loyalty, but the objects of that loyalty were hereditary social classes whose intellectual superiority was neither demonstrable nor relevant.

The examples above illustrate the point that too much ability (or success) may preclude a sense of belonging to any class, even that of an intellectual elite. The more confident and successful a person, the more likely it is that he draws his self-esteem from his own achievements, not from the collective accomplishments of others like himself. Those whose sense of success is based on identification with a group are far more likely to be members of the New Elite. These people *define themselves* as members of that class and their definition of themselves affects their definition of everyone else. It's the window through which they see the world.

It is easiest to view the world through only one window if most of the others have been boarded up. The degree to which one's measured intelligence becomes the basis of his or her self-identity depends on the extent to which other loyalties or roots are rejected. As a general rule, the less reliance on background or roots, the greater the likelihood of self-inclusion in the New Elite. A clean slate invites new scribblings.

Millions of Americans today begin their adult lives with furious erasure. In this regard, the example of Charlene is typical of many well-educated young people who have deliberately sought to divorce the past from their present. In an age of marked social and economic mobility, of the disintegration of neighborhoods, of quick and frequent changes in the places people live, of the erosion of the most basic "root" institutions—family and church—it is for an increasing number of people no longer even a question of rejecting roots: it is a matter of never having acquired roots in the first place. If people derive their identity from the positions to which their measured intelligence has taken them, it is perhaps because there are fewer alternative sources from which they can define that identity at all.

So, the first step is a class awareness. The next is to attach significance to that class—to find and proclaim those things that make it special. This is a natural progression: everyone seeks to extol the group to which he or she belongs. Farmers stress the virtues of the rural ethic. Aristocrats speak of breeding. Members of every group seek to locate the most commendable trait its members share, then emphasize this one aspect of identity to enhance the status of the group and through it their own self-esteem.

With the New Elite, the commendable trait is intelligence. Not for them the argument that city planners are better than plumbers or boasting about one's income. They prefer to emphasize the source of their bounty: measured intelligence.

Jobs, income, lifestyle, and taste were made possible for some individuals because they scored well on tests. (Even those who gained their comfortable livelihoods through nepotism or luck believe this.) This is the focus of the New Elite pride. They like to emphasize not what they have but how they got it. They see themselves as the only class whose position was earned by scientific measurement.

But measurement of what? The New Elite does not doubt the answer: measurement of intelligence, of general ability. It feels that its members have been objectively selected as the "best" in society, that their general intelligence has been proven beyond a doubt. They accept as a given that their clear superiority in the making of all decisions has been unarguably established.

This stems from a misunderstanding of what is measured by intelligence tests. Intelligence tests can be said to be "verifiable"; that is, when one excludes the effects of cultural disadvantage, one can, by correlation with other tests or achievements, demonstrate that IQ tests on the whole provide a roughly accurate tool of measurement. But measurement of what? This question is seldom asked, let alone satisfactorily answered. IQ tests *seem* to measure certain abilities that society rewards; when they score well on those tests, some individuals are rewarded by society. But even assuming that this inherent circularity proves the accuracy of the test, it says nothing at all about the test's *object:* we still don't know what it is that is being measured. It's been said that the only thing an IQ examination really tests is the ability to do well on an IQ examination. The New Elite does not find this observation very amusing. They believe that there is such a thing as "general intelligence," that it can and has been measured, and that those with high scores are generally better able to make correct decisions than those with lower scores. While less a conclusion than an attitude, this is sufficient to verify the test results for most members of the New Elite.

Charlene was told by a test score that she would get better grades in graduate school than almost any of her classmates, which she did. Charlene's husband competed for a very good job against four or five other applicants whose grades were not so high as his own, and he won. Members of the New Elite have observed that test scores accurately predict that certain rewards follow from certain scores. The recipients of those rewards are the least likely to question the appropriateness of the procedures by which they gained them. Because the tests are considered accurate in correlating scores with rewards, they are seen as accurate in equating scores with ability.

Equally significant is the perceived value of quantified proof. People learn that some things can be proven objectively. It can be proven, for example, that water is heavier than oil. It can be accurately predicted that one out of every seven persons born will be left-handed. Educated people have been taught that certitude rests on quantification, that is, if something can be quantified, it can be proved or predicted. It is now widely assumed that intelligence has been quantified. But can something be quantitatively verified even if the numbers have been arbitrarily assigned? Shouldn't the numbers themselves be based on objective reality? While we can ascribe a numerical weight to a liter of water, and that weight can be verified by comparison with other liquids, this is not the case with IQ scores. One can compare those with high scores with those with low ones and demonstrate that the former group will make more money, receive higher grades, gain higher status, and so forth. But jobs and grades have no absolute meaning in themselves; they represent certain values and skills that society has chosen to reward. They may be the rewards only for certain aspects of intelligence. The assignment of numbers to intelligence does not alter this fact; it obscures it. People continue to accept the fact that someone with an IQ score of 140 is "smarter" than someone with a score of 110, just as they accept that a day when the temperature is ninety degrees is warmer than a day when the temperature is only sixty-five.

Members of the New Elite believe not only that their general intelligence is superior to everyone else's, but also that this can be objectively demonstrated. The New Elite derives the "proof" of its superiority from numbers that have been arbitrarily assigned, assuming from those numbers both the need and the right to govern—to make the basic societal decisions that determine the conditions under which everyone lives.

However, most of the great issues facing society are not resolvable by objective proof. One can argue eloquently the merits of one form of taxation over another, or the desirability of some foreign intervention or a certain distribution of wealth. A society may become convinced that prostitution should be legalized or that God exists. But these things cannot be proved objectively by a process so certain that it is followed by a cessation of debate. It is precisely because one cannot "prove" the superiority of one policy over another that some societies permit the resolution of issues through the processes of majority rule. The welter of argument and the weighing of values are submitted to the people and, it is hoped, the policy they select will be better tailored for society's needs than the alternatives. By definition, that policy will enjoy majority support and thus contribute to the general stability of society. Sometimes, the majority will select the wrong policy, but that is a calculated risk; there seems no better way.

The New Elite thinks there is a much better way. Its members don't deny that the great policy questions of the day cannot be decided by some objective formula that vitiates all doubt. They concede that one cannot prove that income should be distributed in a certain way or that prostitution should be legalized. After all, such things are not subject to quantifiable proof. But something else is: their own superiority. This, they feel, can be and has been measured as certainly as the weight of water, and as subject to numerical gradation as variances of heat. Policy itself may not be subject to such objective exactitude, but "general intelligence" is. So, it follows, if one knows precisely who the "smartest" people are, then that is enough for the formulation of public policy. That policy should be decided by the ablest people.

Other elites have wanted their views to prevail, but only the New Elite believes that its views must prevail because the holders of those views are provably superior to the rest of society. If one believes that all this is scientifically shown to be certain, then one believes that the views of the New Elite should prevail on all occasions and at any cost. No tactic is unjustified if it helps enshrine the views of those who know best. Majoritarian institutions are seen as barriers that must be breached, anachronisms from a time before the ablest citizens could be identified. The right of the New Elite to prevail over the majority seems (to its members) as inevitable as the replacement of candle power by electricity—as inevitable as any other scientific advance. And just as the views of the "smartest" must be best for society, so the objections of the rest of society can be discounted because that majority is by definition less able than its objectively selected elite. The emphasis is no longer on which policies are best, but rather on who is best able to decide which policies are best. The search for peers has replaced the discussion of issues in current political activity. The point of governance is not what should be done but who should do it.

This new perception stems not only from the assumption that general intelligence can be tested, but also from the corollary assumption that public policy can be formulated by reason alone. In deciding policy matters, the New Elite implicitly regards rationality as vastly more important than experience. Accordingly, the political battles between the New Elite and the Left Behinds are in large part a contest between the relative roles of reason and experience. Majoritarianism is the obvious preference of those who value the role of experience in the construction of public policy. If experience best defines the needs and hopes of each individual, then the aggregate experience of all people should provide the basis and direction of public policy. It is what Justice Holmes meant when he wrote that "a page of history is worth a volume of logic." But to the New Elite the reverse is true. To them, logic is everything in the world of human affairs, and history is merely the sordid chronicle of its absence. Experience may define what people want, but reason alone can determine what they *should* want.

Their fundamental objection to experience is that everyone has it. And there is no formula, no quantitative means, for proving that one person's experience is more meaningful than another's. One is forced to regard all people as equal. With rationality, however, such leveling can be avoided. It is possible to assert that some people can reason more capably than others. Numbers can and have been assigned to the relative capacity to ratiocinate. Those with the highest numbers will see the clear superiority of reason over experience in the conduct of public affairs. They become more convinced than ever that success in government depends not so much on choosing correct policy but on identifying those select individuals who should be entrusted with the making of that policy.

This is not a matter of metaphysics. The experience-versus-reason polarity, the temporary ascendancy of one viewpoint over the other, has the most direct and dramatic effects on society. In the 1960s, for example, a group of superbly credentialed superstars, of whom McGeorge Bundy may serve as the perfect example, succeeded in altering the direction of American foreign policy. By the rarified application of reason alone, Bundy decided that the United States should become militarily involved in Vietnam. His reasoning was elaborate and profound, and it relied in part on innovative concepts such as a "domino theory" of intensifying loss that could be prevented only by the immediate deployment to South Vietnam of American troops and equipment. Against this glittering analytical construct, much simpler men, including many military officers, could argue only from experience, which suggested that land wars waged in Asia by the West had always ended in failure. Bundy's reasoning prevailed, and the rest is history—for those who still believe that history is relevant.

It is significant why Bundy's views prevailed. His policy was adopted partly because his brilliance was indisputable. His intellectual credentials were breathtaking: summa cum laude at Groton; the first Yale student to get three perfect scores on his college entrance exams; dean of Harvard College at thirty-four; eloquent in discourse and devastating in debate. He surely impressed and reassured the president whom he served, Lyndon Johnson, a man not noted for modesty but curiously insecure in the supposedly arcane realm of foreign policy and all too aware, despite his very considerable gifts, of the contrast between the Ivy League laurels of his advisers and his own background at Southwest Texas State.

The critical anecdote that reveals Johnson's attitude is recounted in David Halberstam's *The Best and the Brightest*. Halberstam relates that Johnson, as vice president, attended the first meeting of the Kennedy cabinet and was overwhelmed by the luminosity of its members. "Stunned by their glamour and intellect, he had rushed back to tell [House Speaker Sam] Rayburn, his great and crafty mentor, about them, how brilliant each was, that fellow Bundy from Harvard, Rusk from Rockefeller, McNamara from Ford. On he went, naming them all. 'Well, Lyndon, you may be right and they may be every bit as intelligent as you say,' said Rayburn, 'but I'd feel a whole lot better about them if just one of them had run for sheriff once.'"

It is instructive that the most thorough account of the decisions that led to Vietnam is titled *The Best and the Brightest*. Its author concluded that "if those years had any central theme, if there was anything that bound the men, their followers and subordinates together, it was the belief that sheer intelligence and rationality could answer and solve anything."

There is another step to membership in the New Elite: the demand for power. The New Elite believes that if a particular group is able to make the best decisions, then its decisions should be followed. If one group knows best, it should govern; its will alone should prevail. They consider the need for majority sanction outmoded, a leftover from the days before ability could be precisely measured. From now on, they believe, the New Elite alone should determine the course of society, should be able to make the decisions for everybody else. To believe this is, of course, to reject the requirement of majority rule. That requirement, and the structures and traditions that support it, must be avoided and evaded until they are no longer meaningful. To this end, the New Elite has already transformed and weakened much of our political system, and it has made vast inroads toward the dominance of our society. The goal of this dominance is not the enactment of any particular ideology but the enthronement of certain personnel. It is rule by the New Elite for its own sake. The New Elite is so certain of its superiority that its sole political objective is to see its members placed in positions of power so that all future governance will be safeguarded. It seeks to recognize its own and guarantee to them the right to govern all.

Of course, this is not always easy. Recognizing one another requires some skill. It can even be a formidable task. People can't walk up to strangers and ask what their SAT scores were; even if they could, test scores and grades alone are very fallible guides to recognition of the New Elite. What the New Elite seeks is not really those of high intelligence; that category is too broad. Instead, the search is for allies. Intelligence is the putative attribute that supposedly gives credence to the claims of the class, but the class itself is what really matters to its members, and the signs of that class allegiance are the true beacons of its search.

Some of those signs are easier to spot than others. As mentioned earlier, a reliable clue is the way people earn their living. Occupation is considered a good index of membership in the New Elite. Certain kinds of jobs suggest the probability of class allegiance. Any work that requires "objectively" tested ability suggests the new class status.

Life is much simpler when one believes all this. A person's "intelligence" may be deduced from the position in society that that person has attained.

One need only apply the New Elite's threshold test. Once that test has been met, eligibility then depends on inward things: attitude, identity, the level of rejection of one's roots.

Membership is definitely not a question of how much money someone has. The membership test for the New Elite is only incidentally economic. In fact, too much money may serve as a disqualifier—and not only in the case of inherited wealth. For example, Texas oil millionaires are never seen as members of the New Elite by those who are members. An associate professor of history makes a good deal less money than the president of a department store, yet the former may meet the achievement test easily while the burden of proof may hang heavily on the latter. The New Elite recognizes intelligence partly in terms of success, but it has its own strict notions as to what constitutes the proper success—that based on testable skills. Academia and the professions provide the most obvious examples. The wrong kind of achievement, the great disqualifier for the New Elite status, is success based on the marketplace rather than on the test score.

This is because the marketplace is the forum of economic majoritarianism. Success there depends on appealing to the largest number of people. Most owners of small businesses are therefore economic majoritarians. Their rewards are not bestowed as the result of a certain score but are won in the marketplace. The same is true for merchants, manufacturers, salesmen, and some people in advertising. These fields are regarded with great suspicion by the New Elite. The owner of a chain of hardware stores might conceivably be accepted as a member, but only after considerable demonstration that his true values were quite different from those of his fellow merchants (It's unlikely that they would be; those who succeed in the marketplace have the best reason to believe in the good sense of the general public.)

It is noteworthy that these careful distinctions of work and wealth are almost unrelated to the subject of IQ. The self-made businessman might very well be more intelligent than the associate professor of biology, and his superiority might be independently evidenced even by test scores and college grades. This is obviously true in a great many such comparisons—perhaps in most—but it is of no matter to those who see themselves as the New Elite. Their loyalty is to the categorical manifestations of testable meritocracy, and not to individual examples of intelligence itself. Theirs is a class loyalty. They resent, perhaps most of all, the obviously gifted businessman, because his success is an evasion, or even a denial, of their basic loyalty, which is the source of their own identity. By prospering in the marketplace, to a degree greater than they can achieve as his employees, he causes others to participate in that majoritarian forum and to see it as a valid determinant of where ability truly lies.

The relation of status to jobs is very complicated. The distinctions maintained by the New Elite are various and subtle. For example, while the practice of law ranks highly with the New Elite, there are gradations. An attorney who practices tax law is more likely to be seen as a peer than is a litigator. While it is impossible to demonstrate that either of these specialties requires more general intelligence than the other, it is generally thought that the skills of the former are the more nearly related to testable qualities, such as analytical ability or the capacity to analogize. The trial lawyer may well possess these abilities to the same degree, but they necessarily are directed toward persuasion of a jury, and success depends on winning the minds and emotions of a randomly selected panel of citizens. Such direct interaction with the general public vitiates the trial lawyer's credentials in comparison with other members of the bar who work with paper, and not people. Theirs is considered a loftier pursuit, the results of which depend on objective criteria, such as reasoning and deduction. It is assumed that success won by the consensus of a jury is inherently less defensible.

This sort of distinction permeates the whole spectrum of employment. As described earlier, the basic New Elite test for the ranking of job status appears to be based on how removed a person's work is from ratification by the public. A scientist's progress can be measured by objective, neutral principles; there need not be a human factor at all. Bankers, however, occupy a somewhat perilous place in the New Elite hierarchy. While it is conceded that they deal rationally with the allotment of funds and the analysis of projects, much of their work involves the granting of loans, which depends in part on adroit assessment of human nature. Investments, too, are ultimately related to success in the marketplace, to appeals for public favor. This taint is noted, regardless of how well educated and rational a banker may be or how much distance from the masses he maintains in his daily conduct. In addition, there is the overpowering fact that bankers believe in the power of money. Power to the New Elite is a task awarded to the measurably able. Dealing with and affirming the connection of power with wealth are antithetical to their concept of how the world should work.

There is no formal chart that ranks the New Elite status of each job. And even if there were, people don't casually describe what they do with enough specificity to permit exact placement on such a chart. In any event, job description alone can't qualify one for the New Elite, any more than can a certain income or an IQ score. This kind of information is helpful but not dispositive. Attitude is what is all-important; knowing someone's educational background, job, and salary is helpful only because they suggest what that person's attitude might be.

That's why style is of particular importance. The lifestyle of the New Elite is the most reliable guide to its members' mutual recognition. Clothes and cars and food and countless nuances of speech and decoration proffer all the clues in the search for shared identity. This is an area of manifold subtlety, and it is often impossible to distinguish the New Elite lifestyle from that of most members of the upper–middle class. But there *are* two factors that meaningfully distinguish the New Elite: the stringent avoidance of any item or conduct that enjoys wide public popularity and the deliberate adoption of lifestyles that are at variance with one's own roots.

Lawyer A attended the same schools and received the same high grades as lawyer B. Their professional duties and salaries are identical, and each earns $250,000 per year. Yet their lifestyles identify lawyer A as a member of the New Elite and lawyer B as merely a professional man with a good income. Lawyer B lives in a large new house in an affluent suburb. His home is filled with appliances and gadgets, and he owns two cars, both large and both American. In these matters, he has attempted not to reject the standard aspirations of American society but to amplify them. Lawyer A's house is nearly one hundred years old, and the considerable sums he lavished on it were directed to restoring as much of its original style as possible. In a society in which the new and modern and gleaming are popular standards of domestic ambiance, an older home, redolent of a past era, is divergent enough to appeal to the New Elite. Lawyer A removed all the wall-to-wall carpeting that came with his house and covered the oak floor sparingly with throw rugs. This was not entirely an aesthetic decision. In the middle-class household in which lawyer A was raised, wall-to-wall carpeting was considered highly desirable, a mark of affluence and status. Lawyer A, consciously or not, is rejecting a value of his parents and thereby displaying the attitude of the New Elite. Lawyer B has wall-to-wall carpeting—all wool. His parents' carpeting was synthetic. He is not rejecting his parents' values but trying to exhibit a greater attainment of the things that they valued.

There's no one thing that makes all the difference—be it carpeting, clothes, or manner of speech. But all the little things together constitute a style, changeable, imprecise at best as a key to certain ranking, but still by far the most available source of information by which the New Elite can surmise who really belongs. Each stylistic detail works to affirm or deny the basic definition of the New Elite.

That definition has several components, of which the easiest to convey through style are high measured intelligence and the rejection of roots and tradition. With regard to the former, intelligence itself is less easily communicated than is the evidence of higher education. It is helpful to know what degrees one has obtained and from which institutions. While this information is seldom blurted out with introductions, the general impression of one's educational attainments can be conveyed in numerous ways: through vocabulary and expression, the dropping of phrases, and allusions to certain topics, titles, and facts. Clothing and even hair styles, the adornments of one's person and one's home, and a stated preference in films or restaurants provide imperfect but frequent inklings of the influence of academia.

The New Elite seems equipped with radar in identifying its fellow class members. The clues are not really the obvious stereotypes, such as chardonnay versus beer. (The New Elite drinks plenty of beer—so long as it's imported or lo-cal.) Many lifestyle choices are merely economic indicators and often unrelated to new class allegiance. That's why radar is needed, and it works on everything—shoes, ties, churches, cars, synonyms, jewelry, attitude (disdain is New Elite and the look of troubled concern is *very* New Elite), neighborhood, and so on, some signals too faint to receive and others as blatant as lawn signs or bumper stickers.

While it is not difficult to give the impression that one is well educated, the New Elite must simultaneously display a rejection of roots. This can be complicated. Millions of Americans earn degrees each year, an achievement so commonplace that now the ultimate rejection of middle-class values might be the decision not to receive a college degree. Some who have chosen this negative option are the ultimate members of the New Elite. The bright children of comfortable backgrounds who scorn both higher education and careers are not really abandoning their identity with the new class, they are affirming it. They may choose to wear overalls instead of tweed, to work with their hands in restaurants or at kilns, to reject rationality itself and retreat into mysticism or drugs. In such cases, the denial of grades or money or professional status or reason is a denial of middle-class values and not of superior status, of roots and not of ability. The fact that they don't have to "prove" that ability in school or at jobs shows how confident they are about possessing it.

In fact, this most recent generation of the New Elite is the most honest in acknowledging what they see as the real source of its identity: heredity. They assume they have inherited from parents (whom they may despise) superior mental ability. Theirs is a natural superiority, confirmed by tests and conveyed to them repeatedly by teachers and family. And since superiority is for them so certain, there is no reason to *do* anything with it. There is no need to prove anything further by achievements. Indeed, to do so would be to suggest that superior status should be earned through deeds instead of simply existing as the natural inheritance of the gifted few.

However, most members of the New Elite do not yet share this perception. They see themselves as having been born superior, but for them there's an intermediate step between that perception and its acknowledgement by everyone else: performance, the actual accomplishment of the tasks that society rewards. Perhaps this is a temporary phase in the evolution of the New Elite. Future generations, like the handful of harbingers already among us, may dispense entirely with the requirement of performance. All that will be necessary will be the fact of their measured intelligence. Eventually, even that may be regarded as irrelevant, and inherited class status will be seen as the ultimate test.

But this is only speculation. The present disposition of the New Elite is quite different and very clear. Its claims to superiority rest on IQ scores and grades and—most markedly—on the jobs and skills and status and style that have resulted from these measurable indicia. The positions these people have attained are to them the proof that their test scores were right in the first place. What the scores and status together affirm—to them—is a natural superiority in the ability to reason. From there, it is but a short step to the next position—where the important decisions in this world must be made by them and them alone—and they have taken that step.

They have been working toward just that goal. In doing so, they have transformed the structure and the scope of our democracy, and they have already destroyed many of the most fundamental underpinnings of our system of majority rule.

FOUR

What They Want: The Death of Politics

Everyone knows that something is wrong. People find it hard to articulate, but the feeling is almost universal. There is the sense that nothing works anymore, that events are beyond control, that things just happen. This feeling, unique in our national experience, is probably best described by the word *helplessness*. There is a pervasive fear that we have lost the means to effect our own destiny. This is not a sense of personal failure; it has to do with the society as a whole. Our society seems like a rudderless ship: there is no way to steer it or alter its course, it is without captain and crew, and we are trapped as its passengers.

This problem is often thought to be political. Surely, the most apparent change *is* in the area of politics. Each new poll confirms the worst. People feel alienated from their institutions and the government seems distant, apart. Unresponsiveness above produces apathy below. An alarming number of citizens no longer bother to vote. Candidates for public posts at every level appear interchangeable and mediocre. In fact, so many choices are between the lesser of competing evils that the very concept of choice is now eroded. The level of discourse is dangerously low. There is no focus at all to public issues. All that's left is anger.

Other times have seemed bad, too, but surely this is different. The conflicts of the past seem preferable to the utter resignation of the present. This may be the quietest crisis in our history, but in many ways it also is the worst.

Perhaps the most disturbing aspect of this crisis is the failure to pinpoint its cause. In fact, the most frequent explanation one hears is actually just the opposite of the truth. The standard line places all blame on the political process. Yet politics has been the victim, not the cause, of the present problem. We're in the mess we're in because the political process has been abandoned. That process, however imperfect, provided the link between the people and their government, between our hopes and our future. And when that process was rejected, the link was severed. Politics is not killing us; on the contrary, politics is dead.

It isn't only the old politics that's dead, but *all* politics. What was recognizable and workable in our political structure has vanished. Political parties are hollow shells. The lines of communication are down. All the innards of our system of self-government have been disparaged and dismantled. In short, there is no politics anymore.

Its death was not accidental. Someone caused it to happen. The destruction of our political process was executed by those who had the most to gain from its demise: the New Elite. The growth of this new class coincided with, and was responsible for, the decay and expiration of politics as the mechanism for popular consent.

This was necessary in order for the New Elite to expand its power. If the New Elite were to rule, then the majority could not. The institutions that made it possible for the majority to rule had to be destroyed. Elections, parties, candidates, attitudes—all the apparatus of popular consent—had to be changed beyond recognition.

And this is just what has happened. It's what accounts for the panic and confusion that we feel as a people today. Of course, the destruction of our political system is not a deed that could be done openly. It simply would not have been tolerated. So it had to be accomplished by stealth.

No one proposed a law abolishing elections. But some people could—and did—so change the way we do things that elections are deprived of meaning. No one dared seriously to demand an end to political parties. But through radical alteration of both rules and attitudes, both parties have nearly ceased to exist. And most preposterous of all would be to decree that people should have no say in their own governance. Yet that is what we've come to—close enough, at any rate, for the loss to be felt all around us, though its causes are not yet obvious.

The causes must be recognized, though, and soon, if there is any hope of reversing what has happened. The cure lies in perception. We have to see what has happened, and why. The political goal of the New Elite is very simple: the transfer of political power to the New Elite. This has very little to do with issues or with the advancement of any philosophy or cause. It does have to do with who is fit to govern—as decided by the New Elite. Since members of the New Elite believe that intelligence can be measured and that it is now possible to know who the "ablest" members of society are, they see no reason why decisions should be put to the less able (the majority). What they want is to rule by themselves.

Their problem is democracy. We transfer power through free elections in which all adults can vote. By tradition and law, the majority rules. The candidate with the most votes wins. But who decides who the candidates will be? That is the critical question. Traditionally, the answer has been very simple. Political parties choose the candidates—two parties, usually, and sometimes, for a brief while, three. Each nominates a candidate, and the public chooses between them.

To the New Elite, political parties are both the barrier and the opportunity to power, the Maginot Line of majority rule. Parties are a barrier because since there are only two of them, winning an election means attracting a majority of the voters. But this also affords an opportunity, because the two parties provide the only alternatives between which the voters can choose. If one or both of the parties can be captured, alternatives can be dictated to the voters; hence, sanction by the majority has no meaning. If the voters can choose between only the offerings of the New Elite, or if one "majority" party is controlled by the New Elite, then the majority no longer rules. The Maginot Line can be breached.

The opportunity has been taken. The effort has been under way for quite some time; though it is not yet completely successful, enormous inroads have been made. The parties may not yet be wholly captured, but they are gravely weakened. The barrier to New Elite political control is almost down.

The most serious damage has been inflicted by changes in the rules under which the parties operate. It is impossible to overstate the impact of this tactic. Yet because the subject of rules, particularly those governing a political party, is of very little interest to most citizens, many of the changes have gone unnoticed. The press has directed its vigilance toward candidates and elections; it seldom mentions the inner workings of the parties. As a result, changes in the rules constitute the great unreported political story of recent times—and one unmatched in our tradition of self-governance. It is a story of the reversal of that tradition, performed covertly and from within. It is a story that concerns both parties, although we shall focus on the Democratic Party, where the rules were more profoundly changed.

The most important rule change was the abolition of "winner take all." In its place, a whole new system of proportional representation was established. To most observers, it seemed like an enlightened step at the time. It is important to note just what time that was. The year 1968 marked the peak of political protest against the war in Vietnam. In the following years, popular support for that cause would grow, but 1968 saw its sharpest political focus. The source of that focus was the Eugene McCarthy campaign. It offered opponents of the war the opportunity for immediate change, peace instead of war. (By 1972, each party was claiming that it could achieve peace more quickly.) The McCarthy campaign was not outside the political process. It was directed toward a very specific political goal—the selection of enough delegates to the Democratic National Convention to win the nomination for Senator McCarthy.

In those days, most delegates to a national convention were selected at state conventions. Some states, like New Hampshire, had presidential primaries, where the delegates were elected at the polls, but most states—thirty-seven out of fifty—did not. It seems so far away now, but as recently as 1968, national convention delegates generally were chosen by the parties, not the public. State parties chose these delegates in several ways. Some followed a precinct caucus system, where every party member could take part, and others relied on appointment by party or state officials. Others had primaries that were not binding; they were an index of how the voters felt, but the delegates selected need not reflect those voters' wishes.

These arrangements caused considerable resentment. When the fervor of the McCarthy movement resulted in a spectacular victory in a state primary, the joy of the activists was intense. But later, when it came time to pick the delegates, that joy turned to rage. In Pennsylvania, for example, McCarthy won the primary overwhelmingly, but nonetheless, many of Pennsylvania's delegates were pledged to Hubert Humphrey. McCarthy supporters saw this as a grave injustice, a rejection of the popular will. What right did a party chairman, or even a state convention, have to disregard hundreds of thousands of ballots? It wasn't fair.

Or was it? Public opinion polls at that time were unanimous in finding that more Democratic voters favored Humphrey than McCarthy. This was sometimes true even with a state where McCarthy received the most primary votes. If the polls were accurate, there could be only one explanation for what was happening: the primaries were not attracting a perfect cross section of the general electorate. Indeed, this was—and continues to be—the case. There are far fewer voters in a primary than in a general election. And those who vote in a primary tend to be much better educated than the electorate as a whole. Many rank-and-file members don't care to take an active role in selecting their party's nominee, even when they have a preference as to who that person should be. Their abstinence or confusion or laziness—if that's what it is—is not to be commended. But it remains a fact: a great many voters, particularly the least educated, choose not to vote in primaries, and a disproportionate share of the better-educated voters do turn out.

It is not surprising, then, that many of those educated voters looked with favor at the primary results. This was to change very greatly, but in 1968, they saw much to recommend the primary system. It seemed to produce the result that they wanted. It became for them the test of what was right. They claimed that primaries represented "the people" because the primaries represented people like themselves. If the party leaders didn't always choose the candidate who had done best in the primaries, then the party leaders were wrong. In fact, the party system was wrong. It would have to be changed.

Before the year was out, the reform movement had begun within the Democratic Party. Its goal was to completely change the way that party operated by drastically changing the rules. In this regard, the reform movement was astonishingly successful. By 1972, it had accomplished its goal.

The most hated rule was that which permitted "winner take all." This practice had particularly outraged the McCarthy delegates, and with good reason. Let us say that a state party convention was entitled to select twenty national delegates. At that state convention, 51 percent of those voting favored Humphrey and 49 percent supported McCarthy. Under winner take all, the Humphrey forces would elect all twenty delegates. Not eleven, or even fifteen—but all twenty. The McCarthy delegates got nothing at all (except in those places where *they* had 51 percent and could take all the delegates). In state after state this happened and, to put it very mildly, the losers did not like it at all. They swore to do away with the hated system, so they came up with something that they thought would work much better.

The reform movement introduced a system of proportional representation in place of winner take all. It was simple and very attractive at first. Each side would get its fair share. A group that had, say, one-third of the votes at a state convention would be guaranteed one-third of the delegates to be elected. No one could possibly argue with that.

And very few did. Once the battles of 1968 were over, the party regulars in several states offered surprisingly little resistance to the clamor for reform. They agreed to much that was proposed; it seemed a small price to pay for the return of intraparty peace, and the incessant cries of the media for party reform would at last be stilled. And the reforms didn't seem so bad to most of the regulars. Proportional representation was a mouthful to pronounce, but when all was said and done, what harm could there be in giving each side its fair share?

The harm, it turned out, lay in figuring out exactly what that share would be. This was anything but easy. If each side was to get *exactly* its fair share, very complex procedures would be needed. Formulas would have to be devised. More rules were needed. And if those new rules were good enough for state conventions, they were good enough for county conventions, too, and for precinct caucuses, and for every gathering, however small, of party people concerned with party business. Every contingency had to be anticipated. A group could never be allowed even one more delegate than its fair share. Exactitude was the goal, and to reach it the rules grew in number and the search for numerical perfection became even more refined. What if a group was entitled to more than six delegates but fewer than seven? The calculators clicked, and the concept of a *half* delegate was born and codified in still more rules.

The best-educated voters—lawyers and teachers, those with verbal skills and advanced degrees—may have understood all these new rules. Many others did not. And so it came to pass that many ordinary party workers grew confused. A county convention composed of farm families who had known one another all their lives found it impossible to sit down together and choose their own representatives. In the past, this had been very easy—an enjoyable way to discharge one's civic duty. Everyone had simply gathered together in a church basement or Farmer's Union hall and selected the best from among themselves—the hardest workers for the party, the ablest, the most trustworthy—to represent the values of the rest. Suddenly, it was very different. At the start of every meeting, the first order of business was the reading of the rules, which went on for quite some time. And when it was over, the participants were confused. It all seemed so difficult. You couldn't just vote for your neighbor; you had to go through a lot of procedures first, to guarantee proportionality, to ensure that mathematical justice would be awarded to each side.

And therein lay another problem, more disturbing to the troubled farmers than the incomprehensible rules: because the rules were set up to give each side its fair share, they required that there *be* sides. You couldn't apportion things fairly if there was nothing to apportion. You couldn't divide things up with justice if no division existed. The rules had been written with division in mind—the great schism of 1968—so they not only reflected division, they required it. You could no longer get together as a unified whole and select your delegates. The rules didn't permit it. You had to choose up sides. A division of the house was required.

But what if nothing divided the farmers gathered in their hall? What if there was no presidential race on which to take sides, no issue such as the war to split them into opposing camps? No matter. To give each side its fair share, you had to have more than one side. The rules demanded it.

People being very resourceful, divisions were found. Everyone might agree on the candidates for president and governor and congressman, but if there was disagreement on whom to run for county commissioner, there was an opportunity to choose up sides. So minor disagreements within the party became the basis for structural disunity.

Nor were those divisions limited to candidates. The rules provided for proportionality with regard to issues as well. People could choose sides on any issue of the day—price supports, a proposed nuclear power plant, wage and price controls, and so on. Each ideological position was entitled to its fair share. And, as with candidates, if no division was at first apparent, one could eventually be found. Local political units whose members agreed on war, peace, taxes, and the draft could be (and were) divided into opposing camps on the question of how many motorboats should be allowed into a nearby wilderness area. The way was paved for single-issue politics.

This produced a profound change in grassroots politics. The basis of political organization was no longer those things that unified people but those that divided them. Intraparty fights were no longer the exception—they were the rule. And with the encouragement of acrimony came a retreat from the quest for compromise and accommodation. Previously, those who favored a candidate or a cause strove to attract others to their side. This was now unnecessary. Under the new rules, it was difficult for any side to be totally excluded, for it was assured of some representation. The need to attract converts in order to survive was gone. And with it went the arts of persuasion, the practice of each side giving up something in order to achieve a slate or a platform that all could support. Consensus, and with it a unified sense of the whole, had disappeared.

That was just fine with members of the New Elite. They had never approved of compromise anyway. Compromise was for those who weren't absolutely certain they were right. If a group feels that it knows better than any other group what is right and what ought to be, why should the purity of that vision be compromised? To do so would be to let all the people in on decisions that their betters could well make for them. In the political arena, compromise is based on the assumption that every citizen has valuable insights that, when pooled, produce a stronger result. But when one group is certain of its superiority, it chafes at diluting its platform or accommodating its candidates for a necessity so base as the winning of majority support.

That necessity had been abolished by the new rules. Now it was possible to participate in politics without compromise of any kind. As a result, parties were deprived of legitimacy with their traditional voters. Candidates who represented a faction, not a party, began to emerge; platforms were written with few planks that seemed aimed at attracting a consensus. The New Elite had changed politics from a majoritarian forum to a new process in which the majority view could not be represented, nor indeed even found.

The legacy of the new rules was confusion, divisiveness, and an inability to compromise ideological purity. To this was added the introduction of quotas—sometimes de facto—for the selection of delegates by specific categories. The process grew more and more rigid. The meetings lasted longer and longer. The farmers left their county convention near dawn, confused and frustrated. Many vowed never to return. After covering the 2004 precinct caucuses in Iowa, Philip Gourevitch was moved to write in the *New Yorker* (Feb. 2, 2004) that "if an election in a Third World country—let's say, Mozambique—were conducted like an Iowa caucus, it might well be condemned by international monitors as a gross human-rights violation."

All of this happened in the name of reform. Fairness had been the ostensible goal. It was more fair, some said, to achieve perfect proportionality in representation. But was it fair to deprive ordinary citizens of a process they could understand? Was it fair to sacrifice comprehensibility to some ideal of mathematical exactitude? Was it fair to preclude a system in which people could work out their differences together? Was it fair to substitute the certainty of faction for the goal of unity? Was it fair to assume that the rights of a political minority could be protected only through the abolition of majority rule?

Fairness had not been the only banner of reform. Openness was a catchword, too. All the new rules were supposed to make things more open. The natural question is: Open to whom? The claim, of course, was that politics would be more open to everyone. The facts suggest otherwise. The reformers used the language of popular consent, but the results show a diminution of that consent. There was much talk of drawing in the poor and disadvantaged, but those were precisely the groups who found the new procedures so difficult. A door was opened wider to a place where fewer cared to go. Increasing numbers of people found political participation too difficult to understand, too acrimonious, too divorced from their own concerns. So they stopped participating.

But others were encouraged by the new procedures. Those whose views on candidates had never found broad acceptance were delighted at the guarantee of representation. Those with parliamentary training and verbal skills reveled in the lengthy deliberations. Those whose professional careers did not require awakening at dawn were more amenable to lengthy evening meetings. The New Elite was very pleased with all the changes. Things truly were more open—for them. What had been done in the name of the people was in fact an exclusion of the people; the only group who actually benefited was the New Elite. And as more and more ordinary citizens dropped out of the process in puzzlement or disgust, the role of the New Elite increased. As fewer people participated, the voice of those who stayed was given greater representation. They called it their fair share.

It all happened very swiftly. By 1972, the Democratic Party was able to nominate George McGovern for the presidency. The convention that bestowed on him the nomination of the nation's largest party boasted that it was more open, more representative, more fairly selected than any in our history. Yet the number who actually voted for McGovern in November was shockingly small. If indeed the process had become more representative, why did so many millions desert their party's choice and guarantee the election of Richard Nixon? Because, to a significant degree, the change in the rules had deprived the Democratic Party of legitimacy with its voters. Neither candidates nor platform were chosen with the goal of winning broad support—and so they did not win it. But it was not merely a candidate who lost. It was the expectation that a party could speak to and for and from a majority of the citizens.

You wouldn't think this one convention could be even more destructive than by nominating a sure loser, but it was. The 1972 Democratic National Convention codified the loony rules that had elected some of its delegates from the more "advanced" states and imposed those rules on *every* state. The problem now was nationalized—and mandatory. The new rules were called "guidelines." If these were actually guidelines, then the Berlin Wall was merely a boundary stone.

The damage caused by the new rules was epochal. The party's traditional role was abandoned, and there came to be a new and ominous reliance on primary elections. In state after state, elected officials saw their parties controlled by an increasingly narrow base. They saw that the rules had been changed to permit, even encourage, the dominance of activists and single-issue factions. It was becoming more difficult for these incumbent officials to stay in office. Traditional party support was eroding. Those who were gaining ascendancy within their own parties were more ideologically rigid and less willing to forgive the compromises that public office requires. The new party activists were perfectly capable of nominating for president a candidate of such limited appeal that hundreds of those who shared his party label on the ballot were dragged down with him in defeat. Panicked, angry, anxious for survival, these officials thought they had an answer. They would switch to the primary system.

It was like a land rush. Throughout the nation, state legislators moved with precipitate speed to change their local laws and provide for primary elections. The political map of the country was swiftly transformed. Formerly, only a relative handful of states had chosen national convention delegates through primary elections. Within a few years, the frightened legislators had finished their work: the great majority of states now had presidential primaries. A very different way of determining who would run for president had been instituted.

The state legislators who brought this about probably felt very proud of their accomplishment—at first. They believed they had served both the public interest and their own with a single stroke. Their own interest was easy to identify. Once the party could no longer select presidential delegates, it was hoped, the new activists would no longer be attracted in large numbers to the party. Unfortunately, it didn't turn out quite that way. With the glamorous lure removed, it was the ordinary party members, not the activists, who stayed away from party affairs. One of the few remaining comprehensible party functions had been the choosing of presidential delegates, and now this too was gone. But the activists remained. State officials had not evaded their scourge.

The public interest was no better served. In establishing primary elections, state officials had boasted that the task of choosing presidential nominees finally would be put in the hands of the people—a victory for democracy. No longer would the voters be faced on election day with the dismal task of choosing a lesser evil. Subsequent events have mocked this claim. Every poll confirms that with the spread of primaries the public has grown increasingly disenchanted with its choice for the presidency. The phrase "choosing the lesser of two evils" has evolved from complaint to fact, the assumed precondition of the quadrennial national ballot. People do not feel that primaries have given them more control; on the contrary, they have never felt so alienated, so incapable of altering their destiny.

This is the big political story of our time, and it is imperative that we understand exactly why it happened. The New Elite did not impose the primary system on us directly, but so altered the parties through rule changes that traditional party leaders themselves switched to primaries as an escape. Every political action brings an equal and opposite reaction; the reaction to the rule changes has been just as disastrous to our democracy as the rule changes themselves.

In *The Future of Freedom,* Fareed Zakaria claims that "the bullet that killed the American political party was the primary election." This is not quite right. The primary election was the ricochet that killed the American political party. The bullet was fired in the very late and humid hours of the Democratic National Convention in Miami in 1972, when the delegates passed "reform" rules that destroyed not only their own party but the other party, too. This because political leaders, seeing party regulars run for the hills and replaced by a handful of snarling extremists, later pushed for laws in which delegates were chosen in state primary elections, rather than by the party itself. That was the ricochet.

The old-time party regulars understood that primary voters would be further from the center than the general electorate, but compared with the clowns now in charge of the process, primary voters seemed a godsend. They were not. In the age of television, primaries became spending contests, with the merits of the combatants almost irrelevant and their views largely unknown. The ricochet from reform was nearly as deadly as the reform bullet itself, and unlike the bullet the ricochet hit both parties.

Democracy requires not only public participation, but continuity, leadership, and structure as well. The people themselves are surely capable of self-governance, but effective self-governance depends on information. There is no way in a pure primary system for the people to inform themselves adequately about the candidates from whom they must choose—not with so many state primaries, anyway, each on the heels of the last. The candidate comes to town for four hectic days of media events and handshaking, after which the people must vote. There are so many candidates, the time is so short, the din so unenlightening, that there's very little basis on which the diligent citizen can make a rational choice. Most voters *are* rational, and so they do the only thing they can. They try desperately to weed out the grosser incompetents from the pack. They know that one of these phantom figures could end up being *president,* the most powerful person in the world. And so they frantically try to figure out who are the most unstable in this pack of office seekers, their first priority being to eliminate such candidates. They're wary of the gravest dangers: the finger on the button, the head in the sand. Primary voters are forced by circumstance to look not for the best candidate but for the worst. They can learn nothing from the thirty-second commercials or the mob scene in the supermarket parking lot, so they watch attentively for slips or mistakes, any hint that suggests disqualification. If a candidate cries or loses his temper, that's it. There's not enough time for the voters to give him or her a second chance.

The candidates who do best in the primaries are those who seem most stable. They are not necessarily the brightest, or the most experienced or thoughtful—just those who appear to be steady. The prize goes to the most unflappable. The situation is perfect for all these candidates who smile benignly at any question, charge, insult, mishap, or attack; and who clearly meet the threshold test of minimal sanity.

It's not a very good way to pick a president. Certainly the public is entitled to something better. The people ought to be able to select a screening committee, not only to weed out the incompetents but to appraise all the candidates carefully, over an extended period. The test should not be limited to a candidate's behavior in a parking lot, but should include how that person has performed throughout a public career. A proper screening committee could analyze each candidate's real stand on real issues—not just the phrases tailored for local consumption—and relate his or her stand to some standard of common values. To really do its job, a screening committee should have worked with the candidates for many years and should be able to judge them from the vantage point of shared experience.

There once were such screening committees; they were called political parties. Now they are no more. They have been altered from within, their functions hurriedly switched to a patchwork system of state primaries. It is true that the screening function performed by those parties was a delegated function, but if government can be representative, why can't politics be as well? Consider the alternative.

Groucho Marx once said that he'd never join a club that would take him as a member. There was considerable wisdom in the jest. He was speaking of the necessity for standards, of the desperate need for a screening committee. If you don't like the screening committee, then get a new one; or reform the committee, but don't reform it out of existence. *Someone* has to screen the applicants, and if no one is permitted to do so, then the final election of new members can scarcely have much meaning.

The ultimate irony of the primary system is that it is being used by the New Elite to further discredit political parties. This gall is divided into three parts. First, the political parties were crippled in their capacity to choose candidates that the people wanted. Second, in reaction to this phenomenon, the job of choosing candidates was thrown to the voters under conditions that made that job impossible. The result was the ubiquity of mediocre and unrepresentative candidates. The public has grown angry at the choices being offered. And now, third, to feed the public's anger, the New Elite has turned to its favorite scapegoat and is ready to place the blame on the political parties. But it won't wash. The reason things are going so badly is not that the parties have failed, but that they have been prevented from doing their job. It's not politics that's to blame, it's the lack of politics. The choice that you don't like is the choice of dozens of primary elections in which the voters have no rational way to make a choice. If the parties hadn't been reformed almost out of existence, if thousands of party regulars could choose from their broad experience, the choice surely would be better. What we have now are candidates with party labels, but they're not the candidates of the parties. They're the candidates of the primaries—which is not at all the same thing as being the candidates of the people. The people were more satisfied when the selection of candidates was made by their political representatives.

Note that the parties are blamed for what they have been prevented from doing, for it's a perfect example of how the New Elite works. Let us summarize once again what the new class does. First, it identifies a majoritarian institution (the political party) that is a barrier to the new class dominance. Then it attempts to control that institution (through rule changes). When the majoritarian institution becomes so weakened by these changes that it is clearly unable to represent the majority will, a populist alternative is developed (the primary system). This alternative is so strongly intended to avoid elite control that most aspects of representative democracy are limited: the people can participate directly but without structure and thus without effect. The performance of this alternative meets with public disapproval (unhappiness with the choice of candidates). Capitalizing on this disapproval, the New Elite heaps more blame on the majoritarian institution that the alternative replaced (the political party), and so further discredits the barrier to its success in a majoritarian society.

There are other examples. In California, political parties became so weak that there was no communicative link between the people and their representatives. As a consequence, neither the governor nor the legislature seemed fully aware of public rage over soaring property taxes. No state action was taken to reduce such taxes, despite a five-billion-dollar state surplus. Pent-up voter frustration finally exploded with the infamous Proposition 13. This alternative was so crude and heavy-handed that it caused many new problems. Now some citizens would blame those problems on the political system— when party politics could have prevented the crisis in the first place. Years later, California's recall of a governor was a clumsy and at best temporary remedy for a failed process. That process had caused both parties to be controlled by extremists. When one party is unable to restrain spending and the other seems prepared to put cameras in our bedrooms, even an outrageously stupid recall law seems acceptable to those who believe in majority rule, and who therefore are represented by neither party. The recall law was absurd, but it was the only choice left to the majority because both parties were controlled by narrow factions. Arnold Schwarzenegger won because he was closer to most voters on the issues than was either state party.

All across America, legislators appear to be out of touch with the voters, because the political parties have been so gravely weakened. Under a properly working political system, the concerns of most voters would become the basis of party endorsement and the problems of the people would become the agenda of government. With parties virtually out of the picture, however, even the most obvious public concerns are unconveyed. Candidates survive primaries and win election by appealing to enough single-issue groups to garner a majority of the votes. But this is not a true majority—there's no one concern shared by its members. There is a series of small mandates to preserve handgun ownership or ban smoking, but there is no big mandate to get to the problems that everyone must face. So most voters, even those who voted for the winners, don't see that their legislators are working on—or are even aware of—the big issues that truly affect us all. That's why we see a movement in so many states for the use of initiative and referendum—the old and very ineffective populist ploy to avoid the need for government altogether. Were we to reach a stage where nothing remained but three or four big referenda each year, the New Elite surely would proclaim a failure of democracy. Of course, it's not really democracy that's failing but all the half-baked alternatives that arose when our democracy was prevented from working. The New Elite gums things up and then points at its own mess to justify further tampering.

It's important to note as well that each step to limit democracy has been made in the name of expanding it. Well aware that our tradition of majority rule still commands affection and respect, the New Elite adapts its tactics to that awareness. It seeks to limit the voice of the people, but it always does so in the name of the people. (In his book, Fareed Zakaria correctly sees that "in the name of democracy we have created a new layer of enormously powerful elites. . . . By declaring war on elitism, we have produced politics by a hidden elite, unanointable, unresponsive, and often unconcerned with any layer of public interest." Unfortunately, Zakaria seems to see this as an inevitable result of a surfeit of democracy, rather than of the deliberate machinations of a new class. His answer to the problem is to rely more on an old elite, an aristocratic class of disinterested statesmen in and out of government. It no longer exists. Groton is turning out another product now.)

The sinister but shrewd Huey Long once was asked whether we'd ever have fascism in America. "Yes," he replied, "only we'll call it antifascism." In a sense, that's just what's happening now. An elite is coming to power under the banner of antielitism. Thus, every change in the rules was made in the name of reform. "Openness" was the battle cry of those who closed things up. What the New Elite extols is precisely what it seeks to destroy. Our most cherished phrases are inverted with a blatancy beyond Lewis Carroll's capacity to mock or Orwell's to portend.

The antidote to all this, of course, is to look at deeds, not words. Change is necessary, but when change is proposed in our basic institutions, the test is what that change will actually do, not what is claimed for it. One of the worst perversions of the word *open,* for example, is in the ominous new push for "open appointments," as when public appointments are to be made by elected officials. Take, for instance, the appointment of judges. Formerly, the appointment of a new federal judge would simply be made by the president after consultation with the senator or senators from the state involved who were also members of the president's political party. This practice is now much derided, and is said to be too "political," as if judgeships have been bestowed purely as reward for past political service. The new alternative is said to be much more "open." Under it, the senator agrees to be guided by a "panel of citizens." The panel screens the names of all judicial applicants and then selects from them a much smaller list from which the senator must then choose. In this manner, it is claimed, judges can be selected by "the people" in a manner free of "politics."

It sounds so right. But when one looks closely at the practice itself, it is much less clear-cut. First, the "political" way of selecting judges was always better than is now claimed. Very few scholars of our judicial system would deny that the caliber of our federal bench has been consistently high. The opportunity for political favoritism was always there, of course, but so was something else that mitigated against its use: accountability. Senators and presidents run for election. Their judicial appointments, if tainted, would be a legitimate campaign issue. Only one party at a time can make a particular appointment, so the other party is quite free to comment on that appointment at will, or even to block its confirmation. The public accountability of those who do the appointing has kept the level of federal judicial appointments relatively high. The lawyers in a given state also have an obvious stake in the ability of their judges, and an angry bar is scarcely an asset to a senator seeking reelection. Those who were appointed in the old way may have been politically active, but they were generally among the most judicially qualified of those in the political arena.

And what, really, does "political" mean? Surely there is something to be said for the appointees of a particular administration sharing its values. The politicians who did the appointing were elected by the people because they stood for certain values. Is it so counter to democratic rule for appointees to reflect in turn the same values that the people themselves have chosen? It can indeed be argued that with judges this should not be the case, but that argument cannot be made by those whose code words are "open to the people." The political process can be the best way of ensuring that appointments *are* open to the people—in a majoritarian society.

The "citizen panels" that are now being set up to make judicial appointments are seldom composed of ordinary citizens. They are usually referred to as "blue ribbon," which means that they are filled with prominent citizens, well educated and often of high professional attainment (though not necessarily in the law). It is probable that they are well intentioned, but this intent could lead merely to the selection of those with similar backgrounds. What guarantee, other than by nomenclature, is there that the "public" interest will be served?

Citizen panels are set up to be "balanced." If there is a woman member, she is said to represent women. A seventy-two-year-old man can be claimed as a representative of senior citizens. And so on. When the panel is fully composed, each member can be pointed to as standing for some specific constituency. All these different constituencies, when added up, are said to represent "the people." But of course they do not. There is a general public good beyond the ken of those who think that enough single-issue parts can make a whole. If the panel members take their labels seriously, the woman is looking for women to appoint to the bench, the senior citizen is vigilant about disqualification because of age, and the businessman and labor leader will be looking for those who share their points of view. If they take their labels *very* seriously, then no one will be interested primarily in finding good judges, because no one's first concern will be the general quality of justice. That would be the people's first concern, of course, but despite all the labels, the people are not being consulted. The citizen panel is in fact the enemy of the people because its members identify either with the upper–middle class, from which most of them are chosen, or with the specific constituencies each is said to represent and whose narrow concerns are often irrelevant to the general task at hand.

The use of such citizen panels has spread. In some states, many of the appointments formerly made by an elected governor have been handed over to panels. This arrangement often can buy some temporary peace for the beleaguered governor. He can assign to the appointing panel the leaders of all the new factions that have been making his public life difficult—and then they can appoint all *their* friends. And since a committee, unlike one lone official, does not run for reelection, it avoids accountability not merely through its corporate state.

These panels, elected by no public vote, are now entrusted with myriad state appointments. If a governor appoints a crony to, say, the state investment board, there will likely be an outcry. When the citizen panel appoints its cronies, there's much less accountability—and much less chance that the appointee represents values sanctioned by the voters. The power to appoint is a lofty one. There has been a great and growing shift in that power away from the mandate of the ballot box.

So much that has happened in recent years has achieved the same result. One might almost posit that the greater the use of the word "reform," the more likely that the public will be deprived of participation. This is even apparent in the realm of campaign financing. A plethora of new laws has changed significantly the role of the contributor. As always, these laws were enacted in the name of rectifying what was in fact a real abuse. There were, indeed, "fat cats" whose huge campaign gifts gave them special favor(s) at court. It was desirable that this be changed, but perhaps the solution is now worse than the problem.

The new class thought that no one should be permitted to give more than one thousand dollars to a candidate. You can see why they found this attractive. Most people couldn't give much at all, and if you put a ceiling on gifts by the rich, then campaign financing would have to rely on you know who. The educated professional class, cats not fat but with a few extra pounds. Campaigns would be financed by people like themselves.

But it didn't turn out that way at all. In the first place, campaign funding is a raging river that is easier to damn than dam. The really big contributors merely diverted their currency into the convenient channel of "soft money." This scandalous arrangement actually raised more huge gifts than before. As with most new class "reforms," the biggest change was to erase accountability. In the second place, the New Elite found it difficult to find the "hard money" contributors on whom they'd placed a ceiling. It took a lot of time to get individual donations of one thousand dollars (since adjusted for inflation). As the most effective way for candidates to do this was to appeal to people already passionately committed to a cause, single-issue fundraising became the norm. And while some of those issues were favored by the new class, a great many others were not. Since then, further "reforms" have been passed, and they are being contested in the courts. Once again, the "cure" will likely only raise the fever.

Once, the strong political party permitted those without great wealth or a famous name to run successfully for office. As the role of the party diminished, however, media campaigning filled the gap. It is a very expensive filler. Now the candidate without private means or public fame can survive only by raising huge amounts of money, and this means turning to special-interest groups. It means supporting narrow issues rather than those of more concern to the majority. The hegemony of single-issue campaign finance is the legacy of the New Elite's effort to dominate financing itself.

The damage inflicted by the New Elite is not part of some sinister plot. High civic motive is often involved. The danger stems not so much from any crafty goal as from the strong proclivity to tinker with our basic institutions. Perhaps the greatest mischief of the New Elite is the rapacity with which it seeks to rewrite our basic rules. Change is often desirable, but it's not always a mandate. The really dangerous notion now abroad in the land is that *everything* should be changed right away—and changed not through convincing the populace of a better course of action but by fiat, through a changing of the rules.

The cause of all this agitation is always a specific event. In every society, things go wrong. When they do, it's only natural to try to prevent their recurrence. This is the point at which the New Elite is most dangerous. Its members are so used to adjusting mistakes on paper that they think they can do the same with everything that disappoints them in life. In public life, this insistence on altering structure reflects disdain for the majority. Other citizens see things they don't like, but their first response isn't to change the rules. If their candidate loses an election, their immediate reaction isn't to restructure the way elections are held. They simply retain the hope that someday their candidate will win. In the practice of majority rule, everyone loses sometimes. Most people are sustained through disappointment, though, by the possibility of being part of a future majority. If your cause is right, others will join it and someday you will prevail.

The New Elite has no such faith. It does not regard the majority as wise enough to come to share the views that one small class already holds. And even if the majority could be persuaded, why should progress be deferred until this comes to pass? Majority sanction is no longer seen as what makes this progress right, only as what makes it happen. If things can happen faster through changing the rules, that's good enough.

The New Elite has been very busy. In the political arena, almost everything now happens under rules that have recently been changed. The worse things get, the worse they will get, as every failure in the innovations is used to justify yet more change. We're coming to the point at which no election will be governed by the same rules as the one that preceded it. We're nearly to the point at which complexity and confusion and rapidly shifting guidelines have shaken most citizens from the hope of participation. Politics is dying, gravely ill from too many transfusions.

What is needed is not an end to change, for that would be as fatal as its careless use. What is called for is skepticism. We would do well to recall Burke's adage that not all change is reform. We must learn to distinguish between the rhetoric of reform and the real thing. The habit of compliance with that rhetoric must cease. The test cannot be only whether there is a problem to be solved; the solution must stand on its own merits, too. People must ask not only "Is something broken?" but also "How will this fix it?" We should apply careful consideration before we permit anything to be done in our name.

The greatest change in the way we govern ourselves as a people has taken place quietly, out of sight of the audience. If the curtain is lifted, the people—as always—will know what to do.

FIVE

Rule by the Courts

Felix Frankfurter was born in Vienna in 1882 and came with his parents to America at the age of twelve. They left behind a wretched life. There was little enough opportunity for almost anyone in the Austro–Hungarian Empire, but restrictions on advancement for Jews were particularly harsh. Education was difficult to obtain, hard work often unrewarded. The Frankfurter family was weary of poverty and bigotry and of limits on life and hope. Like so many others from so many other places, they endured passage to a new land because even the unknown seemed preferable to what they knew too well.

Life in America was difficult at first. There was a new language to learn. Money was scarce. They settled on the Lower East Side of Manhattan, where Felix Frankfurter's father sold linens from a shop in his home and during the summers peddled door to door outside the city.

Felix was, from the moment of his arrival here (and until the last days of his life), a voracious student. His mind was superb, his appetite for knowledge astonishing. School was not nearly enough to satisfy him, so he haunted the New York Public Library. He read everything. He spent at least four afternoons a week in the main hall of Cooper Union.

These opportunities were free of charge, as was his formal education. For reasons now forgotten, Felix Frankfurter was rejected for a scholarship to Horace Mann, a private school in the Bronx, which would probably have led him to Columbia College. So he attended P.S. 25, and then the City College of New York, where there was no tuition and where he received a good education. Many other sons and daughters of immigrants were his classmates; they were bright and as eager to advance themselves as he. Competition was keen and stimulating, but no one outshone Felix Frankfurter. His gifts were remarkable, and very obviously so.

He had always wanted to be a lawyer. After graduation from City College in 1902, he worked in the Tenement House Department of New York City for a year to earn enough money for law school. Almost by chance and without knowing much about it, he enrolled in the Harvard Law School.

It was like entering a new world. His classmates were not the children of immigrants, but part of an American aristocracy. They were urbane, the products of the best prep schools and Ivy League colleges. At first, Frankfurter was terrified—a reaction that soon passed. An extraordinary student, he stood first in his class for all three years and edited the *Harvard Law Review.* He met and dazzled everyone, beginning a lifetime habit of close association with the most accomplished members of his, and several other, generations. He was invited by his professors to their homes, pointed out to visitors, solicited even at that early age by the eminent in several fields.

After graduation, he had his pick of jobs. He worked for four years as an assistant U.S. attorney in New York, serving under the legendary Henry L. Stimson, who became his mentor. When Stimson became secretary of war, Frankfurter followed him to Washington as a legal assistant.

In Washington, as in Cambridge and New York, Frankfurter was magnetic, attracting to him the best minds of his day. His circle was glittering. With some friends, he rented a brick row house on Nineteenth Street and to its doors came supreme court justices, writers, cabinet officials, and artists. A frequent dinner guest was Justice Oliver Wendell Holmes, who had replaced Stimson as Frankfurter's chief mentor. It was common to see them walking together, the tall, white-maned aristocrat and the short young man beside him. They were great friends, and Holmes enthusiastically shared his philosophy as they walked.

Holmes's views on the law and of society itself were distinctive. Though of peerless intellect, he scorned the role of pure reason. He saw progress as evolving from the whims and hopes and experience of all the people. Progress could not be ratiocinated by even the most brilliant scholars, Holmes thought. At the very outset of his great work, *The Common Law,* Holmes left no doubt about his contempt for abstract schemes of social policy. He proclaimed his faith in the will of the people as the proper fulcrum for our common destiny:

> The life of the law has not been logic; it has been experience. The felt necessities of the time, the prevalent moral and political theories, intuitions of public policy, avowed or unconscious, even the prejudices which judges share with their fellowmen, have had a good deal more to do than the syllogism in determining the rules by which men should be governed.

These are remarkable words, even more so for the time in which they were written. It is not pure intellect on which we should rely for social policy but "the felt necessities of the time." Holmes gave great weight to intuition, even unconscious intuition, of the people as the surest guide to a better future. This view was shared and discussed and absorbed as the Brahmin and the immigrant walked the sleepy streets of the capital.

In 1914, Frankfurter returned to the Harvard Law School to teach. Except for one year as visiting professor at Oxford, he remained at Harvard until he was appointed to the U.S. Supreme Court in 1939.

His years in Cambridge were anything but cloistered. The most distinguished people in the world were his visitors, his correspondents, his friends. The powerful, the talented, and the acclaimed arrived with letters of introduction. His soirees on Brattle Street were legendary. Professor Frankfurter's real circle, however, was his students. For twenty-five years, he met and influenced the most promising young scholars in the land. They scattered throughout the country; as many of them rose to prominence themselves, the concentric circles of their teacher's influence spread. Frankfurter knew everybody. The attraction was his intellect. Through ceaseless conversation and voluminous correspondence he reached out from Cambridge to be a dominant part of the elites of his time—social, political, and intellectual.

There is a reason to recount in such detail the kind of life that this man led, for it is relevant to his work. The courts are composed of human beings. Each judge brings a viewpoint to his or her work—a view of what the courts should do. This is of surpassing importance. These views determine what the courts actually do—and how extensive their reach should be.

There are two philosophies about how far the courts should go, and they are at war with one another. One philosophy dominates for a time, only to be supplanted by the other. But whichever viewpoint is ascendant, the effect on all of us is enormous.

There are names for these distinct and opposing schools of thought. Those who believe in the will of the people, who feel that judges should be loath to substitute their own views of public policy for those of a popularly elected legislature, are known as the school of *judicial self-restraint*. "Restraint" is the keyword. It is not that these judges doubt their own wisdom, or that they lack any notion of what path the rest of us should follow. It is simply that they believe the big decisions should be made, if possible, by those whom they most affect, and the wisdom of the people is considered paramount. It is not that the people are always correct or that legislatures never err. But some judges believe that the people have a *right,* through their representatives, to decide things for themselves. These judges draw a distinction between laws that are *reasonable* and laws that are *wise.* If a law is not unreasonable, even if these judges privately dispute its wisdom, they restrain themselves from invoking the Constitution to strike that law down.

Conversely, some judges are *judicial activists,* a species far more aggressive in deciding which laws should be permitted to stand. In many cases, no matter what the public wants, regardless of legislative expression, activist judges have no compunction about using the courts to decide how things should be. No matter whether a law is reasonable, if a judge finds it unwise, it will be struck down; and they consider it a constitutional requirement. At the core of this outlook is a rejection of the role of the people. The popular will, however clear, is not a major factor in upholding or rejecting laws. For a judge to say that a law is "unwise" is to say that he or she obviously knows better than elected legislators what is good for the people.

When Felix Frankfurter was teaching law, the Supreme Court was dominated by judicial activists, most of whom were also quite conservative. This doubtlessly surprises those who are not students of the Court and may suppose that judicial activism and liberalism are the same. In fact, they are not even related. Neither of the contending judicial philosophies is itself inherently either liberal or conservative; rather, they deal with the degree to which the Court permits public laws to stand. Whether judicial intervention, or restraint, has a liberal or a conservative result depends on historical circumstances, that is, whether the laws being passed are "liberal" or "conservative" in nature. This is a constantly changing situation because the political pendulum is never still. So, at one point in history, judicial activists may be seen superficially as liberals; at another they may be seen as conservatives.

During the first third of the twentieth century, the country was quite conservative. Most, though not all, state legislatures reflected this mood. There were progressive movements in the land, which occasionally won enough popular support to help pass innovative social legislation, such as minimum wage laws. However, the Supreme Court declared those laws unconstitutional. This outcome reflected the political philosophy of the Court at that time, which generally was intolerant of government interference with the marketplace. But it was not merely a case of conservative judges striking down liberal laws. To do that, the Court had to rely not only on its own political philosophy, but also on a philosophy of judicial conduct. It also had to announce the right to interfere when it deemed a law unwise. It had to renounce restraint—and that it did.

The Court was not unanimous in this regard. Justice Holmes dissented, as did Justices Louis Brandeis and Harlan Stone. They insisted that the Court should not intrude unless the Constitution specifically allowed it to do so. But while their dissents were eloquent, they did not carry the day. Throughout the 1920s, the Supreme Court, under the leadership of Chief Justice William Howard Taft, regularly declared new economic and social legislation to be un-constitutional. In so doing, the Taft Court was "activist." And liberals, like Professor Frankfurter at Harvard, decried that activism.

Their cries grew even louder after the birth of the New Deal. The political climate had changed completely with the advent of the Great Depression, when the trickle of social legislation became a torrent. The first one hundred days of the New Deal produced an unprecedented outpouring of federal leg-islation—dozens of completely new programs and agencies to combat the economic crisis. Whether these laws were wise or not, they were certainly an accurate expression of a public mood that had transformed the Congress from one party and philosophy to another. An election had been held, and the New Deal seemed to be what people wanted.

Except that the Supreme Court threw most of it out—the popular man-date being of no concern to the judicial activists. The Court succeeded so well in nullifying the New Deal that a frustrated Franklin Delano Roosevelt actually proposed packing the Court with additional members—an awful idea that interestingly enough won little public approval.

Despite the fact that the number of justices stayed at nine, Roosevelt eventually had his way with the Court. In several important cases, Justice Owen Roberts changed his vote, which caused the scholar E. S. Corwin to quip, "a switch in time saved nine." In any case, time was on Roosevelt's side. As the older justices retired or died, Roosevelt appointed their successors and eventually saw a judicial majority that favored his approach. This was, of course, the philosophy of judicial self-restraint. The Roosevelt Court let stand the legislative experimentation of the day. The New Deal could proceed. Re-straint now was considered to be a liberal philosophy.

One of Roosevelt's appointees to the Court was Felix Frankfurter. No one was more consistent in applying the doctrine of self-restraint, and this persisted regardless of the issue involved or his own feelings about a new law. If the peo-ple wanted it, if the Constitution did not specifically forbid it, then the Court, he felt, should not prevent it from being carried out. The important thing, he kept reminding his colleagues, was that legislatures, not the courts, should make our laws. The judge should try not to intrude. Sometimes, this restraint was extraordinarily difficult, even for him. But he did not abandon his convictions.

There is no better example of how strongly Justice Frankfurter adhered to the school of self-restraint, and no better expression of what that school is all about, than his dissent in the case of *West Virginia State Board of Education* v. *Barnette*. This case presents the competing issues in their most dramatic form. And like all such cases, it is linked to the currents of its time, in this instance World War II, when feelings of patriotism were understandably very high. The state of West Virginia had passed legislation that permitted the state board of education to direct all public school children to salute the American flag as part of the regular program of school activities. This directive was offensive to Mr. Barnette, a Seventh-day Adventist and father of a public school pupil. The Seventh-day Adventists held that only the deity could be honored by any gesture such as a salute. To direct such homage to a symbol of the state, such as the flag, was inconsistent with the tenets of their faith. A lawsuit was brought to exempt from the requirements of the salute all whose religious beliefs were thereby violated.

It was not unreasonable to assume the Court would reject the Barnettes' plea. It was by then clearly a Roosevelt Court; the principle of self-restraint was thought to be held by a majority of the justices. A similar flag-salute law had been upheld by the Court, so many felt this state law requiring the salute would also be upheld.

It was not; a majority of the Court agreed with the Barnettes. The Court struck down the law because the religious views of some would be offended by its full enforcement. Even some justices who believed in self-restraint joined in this opinion. For them, the desirability of upholding a reasonable law was outweighed by the claims of religious freedom. They felt so strongly about that freedom that they made an exception to their philosophy.

Justice Frankfurter, however, did not make this exception. His judicial philosophy was put to the hardest possible test, but it survived. The heart of his philosophy was that judges should not substitute their own views for those of elected legislators. He followed that principle. The agony that it cost him to do so is evident in his remarkable dissenting opinion:

> One who belongs to the most vilified and persecuted minority in history is not likely to be insensible to the freedoms guaranteed by our Constitution. Were my purely personal attitude relevant I should wholeheartedly associate myself with the general libertarian views in the Court's opinion, representing

as they do the thought and action of a lifetime. But as judges we are neither Jew nor Gentile, neither Catholic nor agnostic. We owe equal attachment to the Constitution and we are equally bound by our judicial obligations whether we derive our citizenship from the earliest or the latest immigrants to these shores. As a member of this Court I am not justified in writing my private notions of policy into the Constitution, no matter how deeply I may cherish them or how mischievous I may deem their disregard. The duty of a judge who must decide which of two claims before the Court should prevail, that of a State to enact and enforce laws within its general competence or that of an individual to refuse obedience because of the demands of his conscience, is not that of the ordinary person. It can never be emphasized too much that one's own opinion about the wisdom or evil of a law should be excluded altogether when one is doing one's duty on the bench. The only opinion of our own even looking in that direction that is material is our opinion whether legislators could in reason have enacted such a law. In the light of all the circumstances, including the history of this question in this Court, it would require more daring than I possess to deny that reasonable legislators could have taken the action which is before us for review. Most unwillingly, therefore, I must differ from my brethren with regard to legislation like this.

When Mr. Justice Holmes, speaking for this Court, wrote that "it must be remembered that legislatures are ultimate guardians of the liberties and welfare of the people in quite as great a degree as the courts . . ." he went to the very essence of our constitutional system and the democratic conception of our society. He did not mean that for only some phase of civil government this Court was not to supplant legislatures and sit in judgment upon the right or wrong of a challenged measure. He was stating the comprehensive judicial duty and role of this Court in our constitutional scheme whenever legislation is sought to be nullified on any ground, namely, that responsibility for legislation lies with legislatures, answerable as they are directly to the people, and this Court's only and very narrow function is to determine whether within the broad grant of authority vested in legislatures they have exercised a judgment for which reasonable justification can be offered. . . .

The reason why from the beginning even the narrow judicial authority to nullify legislation has been viewed with a jealous eye is that it serves to prevent the full play of the democratic process. The fact that it may be an undemocratic aspect of our scheme of government does not call for its rejection or its disuse. But it is the best of reasons, as this Court has frequently recognized, the greatest caution in its use. . . .

This is no dry, technical matter. It cuts deep into one's conception of the democratic process—it concerns no less the practical differences between the means for making these accommodations that are open to courts and to legislatures. A court can only strike down. It can only say "This or that law is void." It cannot modify or qualify, it cannot make exceptions to a general requirement. And it strikes down not merely for a day. . . . If the function of this Court is to be essentially no different from that of a legislature, if the considerations governing constitutional construction are to be substantially those that underlie legislation, then indeed judges should not have life tenure and they should be made directly responsible to the electorate. . . . Judges should be very diffident in setting their judgment against that of a state in determining what is not a major concern, what means are appropriate to proper ends, and what is the total social cost in striking the balance of imponderables. . . . That which to the majority may seem essential for the welfare of the state may offend the consciences of a minority. But, so long as no inroads are made upon the actual exercise of religion by the minority, to deny the political power of the majority to enact laws concerned with civil matters, simply because they may offend the consciences of a minority, are more sacred and more enshrined in the Constitution than the consciences of a majority. . . .

The uncontrollable power wielded by this Court brings it very close to the most sensitive areas of public affairs. As appeal from legislation to adjudication becomes more frequent, and its consequences more far-reaching, judicial self-restraint becomes more and not less important, lest we unwarrantably enter social and political domains wholly outside our concern. I think I appreciate fully the objections to the law before us. But to deny that it presents a question upon which men might reasonably differ appears to me to be intolerance. And since men may so reasonably differ, I deem it beyond my constitutional power to assert my view of the wisdom of this law against the view of the State of West Virginia. . . .

To strike down a law like this is to deny a power to all government. Of course patriotism cannot be enforced by the flag salute. But neither can the liberal spirit be enforced by judicial invalidation of illiberal legislation. Our constant preoccupation with the constitutionality of legislation rather than with its wisdom tends to preoccupation of the American mind with a false value. The tendency of focusing attention on constitutionality is to make constitutionality synonymous with wisdom, to regard a law as all right if it is constitutional. Such an attitude is a great enemy of liberalism. Particularly in legislation affecting freedom of thought and freedom of speech, much of which should offend a free spirited society is constitutional. Reliance for the most precious interests of civilization, therefore, must be found outside of their vindication in courts of law. Only a persistent positive translation of the faith of a free society into the convictions and habits and actions of a community is the ultimate reliance against unabated temptations to fetter the human spirit.

At first glance, nothing is more remarkable about this dissent than the identity of its author. Felix Frankfurter must have seemed to some a most improbable defender of the popular will. The creator of these paeans of praise to the wisdom of the majority was, after all, an urbane scholar well aware of his own intellectual attainments and unabashedly proud of his distinguished circle of friends. He had been called an elitist, and in some regards this was true. He demanded excellence in his work and in his life, and scorned the slightest abridgment of it. His standards were noble and unyielding. He corresponded with the brightest persons of the day and cultivated the most prominent. He did not lack awareness of his own abilities or position. He was proud, perhaps arrogant, and his life was one of studied cultivation.

But though he was surely a member of the ruling elite, though he may have been an elitist, he was decidedly not a member of what can now be called the New Elite. He was in fact perhaps its most articulate enemy. What kept him in the opposing camp was his passionate belief in majority rule. The fact that he was not, could not have been, and would have fervently opposed being part of the New Elite tells us much about the new class. The most distinctive characteristic of its members is not high intelligence or academic achievement or even a certain rarified lifestyle. If these things were what really mattered to the New Elite, Justice Frankfurter would have been its most prominent member. Instead, he was its passionate foe—because his faith in the people was boundless.

One might well ask why this renowned scholar was so committed to majority rule. Perhaps because he had known life in a country where the people's voice had never been heard. Or because he lost a scholarship and attended public schools. Or because he had lived among working people and had been educated alongside them. Or because he had heeded the wisdom of Holmes during their long walks together. Or because his lifelong study of history had taught him that rule by any elite, however gifted, was a brake on human progress. Or maybe just because he loved this country as only an immigrant can and understood in his heart and his mind just why it is unique.

Whatever the reason, it must have been a terrible effort for Frankfurter to hold against the minority rights of a religious group. He was able to do so because he knew—from both history and logic—that in the long run minority rights are protected best not by generous judges but through the rule of law and that the rule of law itself depends on a people habituated to the processes of self-governance.

When Frankfurter dissented in the *Barnette* case, it was regarded as a very unusual event. The Court was still considered to be in favor of the doctrine of judicial self-restraint; it simply had made an exception to that doctrine, and Frankfurter and the Court's majority were still thought to be of the same general philosophy. And, for a while, this was true. But then the Court began to change, assuming a more activist role. More and more, the Court's majority came to strike down laws with which it disagreed. Frankfurter continued to dissent vigorously and with eloquence; but the trend continued nonetheless and became much more apparent.

The country, too, had changed a great deal. Earlier, the Taft Court's conservative judges had struck down liberal laws. Now, a generally liberal Court was determined to strike down conservative legislation. Sometimes even Frankfurter went along with this approach. He joined with his colleagues— the decision was unanimous—in *Brown* v. *Board of Education of Topeka,* which struck down the "separate but equal" state laws requiring or permitting schools to be segregated by race. Even those who believe in judicial self-restraint are willing to reach out and invalidate a law when that law is so invidious as to obviously offend the Constitution. Frankfurter was not inflexible in the application of his philosophy.

He was consistent, though. Not all laws were so clearly repugnant. And when in doubt, he let them stand. For example, a Texas statute required all labor organizers to register with the Texas secretary of state and receive a permit before they could undertake their organizing activity. A majority of the Court threw out this statute, declaring that it violated the Constitution's guarantees of free speech and assembly. Frankfurter dissented. He was a friend of organized labor, but thought the Court was going too far. He thought that even the First Amendment should be used very cautiously in striking down laws.

And so it went. The Court increasingly nullified legislation on the grounds that it violated constitutional rights. Frankfurter inveighed against this trend. Finally, it came to pass that Justice Frankfurter was no longer seen as the darling but as the obstructor of liberal progress. It became fashionable to say that he had changed. He was frequently referred to as a conservative. Labels became invective, and he was excoriated for the supposed switch in his philosophy.

Of course, he had not changed at all. The Court had changed. The issues had changed. Before, property rights had been challenged by social legislation. Judges who cherished property rights had been quick to nullify the challenge. Now it was individual rights that were challenged by legislatures. Judges who cherished those rights became as activist as any economic conservative from the Taft days in nullifying the challenges to their own beliefs.

Frankfurter was second to none in his reverence for individual rights. But he persisted in subordinating his own views to his respect for the judgments of majority rule. And for this reason, he, and not the country, was said to have changed. He must have agonized at the names he was called. He was probably embarrassed that on the occasion of his seventy-fifth birthday, the most fulsome tribute paid to him on the floor of the U.S. Senate came from that arch-conservative, Senator John Bricker, of Ohio. Considering the source of each, he may well have been more dismayed by the flattery than by the insults.

But his convictions were unchanged. Despite what his critics charged, he was still very much a liberal. He knew that the national concern for personal rights, the new national attitude that condemned his philosophy as conservative, had come about and flourished partly because a handful of brave judges once had insisted on the people's right to decide their own laws. He would not retreat from that neutral principle because of its impact on the specific cases of a later day. He knew that issues changed from one generation to the next, but that if the attitude of judges remained constant in its faith in the people's wisdom, that faith would be rewarded through a progressive uplifting of the national life.

The majority of the new Court did not accept this view. Frankfurter's views had to be voiced in dissenting opinions, then finally not at all. In bad health, he retired from the Court in 1962. He left a Court that was as activist as any in our history, and one that would become even more so.

So entrenched and lauded was the idea of judicial activism that it was no longer restricted to striking down laws that judges thought unwise. Courts began to replace the offending statutes with rules of their own devising. Judges began to substitute their own plans for those of legislatures. Much of this judicial legislation was admirable, and virtually all of it was based on the highest motives. In fact, so much of what was done was so obviously enlightened that few cared to decry the new precedent that judges now, in a very real sense, had usurped the right to make our laws.

The courts went very far, it was conceded, but always for a good cause. In the matter of prison reform, for example, judges did not merely rule that state appropriations to maintain penitentiaries were inadequate; they went on to prescribe just what those appropriations should be and exactly how they should be spent. A federal district judge even ordered that carpeting be installed in a state mental institution. The point is not so much whether this was a "good" decision—the carpet surely improved the quality of the patients' lives—but whether any judge should have been making it. There is only so much revenue available to a state. To spend more public money on one area is to spend less on another. Installing carpeting in mental institutions might mean there is less money for senior-citizen tax relief. Even if the installation of carpeting is the wiser decision, the real question is who should be empowered to make that decision. To Frankfurter, that question had a simple answer: elected legislatures. To the activist judges who followed him, the answer was not so simple: if the legislature didn't do its job "right," then federal judges were entitled to do it themselves.

It is no coincidence that these extraordinary increases in judicial activism coincided with the emergence and growth of the New Elite. It was a trend that suited the new class exactly. Federal judges are not elected, nor should they be. They are appointed and hold their offices for life. It is appropriate that interpreters of the Constitution be removed from the pressures of political life.

And in this arrangement the New Elite saw an opportunity. Lifetime judges, absolutely immune from the electorate, were deemed by the New Elite to be ideal legislators. It wasn't only that they never had to stand for election; equally attractive was their background—they were well-educated professionals in almost every case. How fitting it seemed that such distinguished citizens, dispassionate and free from the worry of popular sanction, should be entrusted not only with interpreting but also actually drafting the new laws of the land.

In point of fact, at no time has a majority of the federal bench been ideologically allied with the New Elite. The former corporate attorneys who continue to make up much of the bench have in many cases a very different outlook than those who cheer their activism. Still, that cheering section is there; less concerned with the ideology of officials than with their academic backgrounds, the New Elite relishes and applauds the idea that laws should be made by scholars, and the growth in judicial activism has had a very effective chorus of support.

And of course it has had a backlash as well. The word *activist* itself has become very significant. Before their confirmation, nominees to the federal bench are required to state just how committed they are to the activist approach. The answer is often fudged. Today, liberals want activists and conservatives do not. Many who loudly insist on the appointment of activist judges describe themselves as political "activists," as well. But how can one possibly endorse both judicial and political activism, unless, of course, political activism has come to mean something different from what its label implies? One who believes in judicial activism can be a political activist only if he or she no longer views political activity as directed toward the achievement of majority support. If one believes that the point of politics is to see that society does what is "right," regardless of what the public thinks or wants, only then can these two forms of activism indeed be reconciled.

The growth of judicial activism was not entirely in response to the heavy demand for it. Other conditions, also traceable to the influence of the New

Elite, helped accelerate the process. The erosion of political parties, the retreat from compromise, the growth of single-issue factions, and the emphasis on style over substance all have served to immobilize the Congress. Decisive action from the legislative branch is much less apparent now than it has been at other times in our history. The political parties of old, large and strong, were a prod and a shield to the legislators they helped elect. They pushed for action; they defended their members against attack. Now, both impetus and cushion are gone. Incumbents see caution as the highest virtue. While the risks of experimentation are very great, not so the rewards. (Congressional incumbents, moreover, need no reward: they cannot be defeated. The House of Representatives has been gerrymandered so that virtually every seat is completely safe for one party or the other. The reader of these words almost certainly lives in a congressional district where the incumbent cannot be defeated in a general election, because the unincumbent party has been limited to numbers that can never prevail. Majority rule means that there is at least a chance that another party can win—thus, the deliberate creation of supermajorities in every district is a denial of democracy in half our legislative branch. It is a mystery why this state of affairs has caused so little comment, let alone protest. It would seem to be unconstitutional.) So little is done by the legislative branch that the pent-up demand for change in society finally finds an outlet in the courts. Even judges not fully attracted to the activist philosophy find themselves legislating from the bench, with the angry explanation that *someone* has to. The Congress has created a void so great, it is not surprising that the courts have moved to fill it.

The worse it gets, the worse it gets. The more likely it is that the courts will legislate, the more attractive it is to the New Elite to keep the Congress from doing so. The nonelected alternative seems to them so much more desirable. So long as this vicious circle persists, the legislature does less and less, and the courts do more and more. In the history of this nation, the courts were never even remotely as activist as they are in our time. The judicial pendulum always swung from activism to restraint and back again. For a long time now, the pendulum has seemed stuck on the activist side. This state of affairs is cheered by the new class. Is this really in their interest? Will they want the court to remain activist when a majority of its members are conservative?

It very well might. The fight on the Court is not between "liberals" and "conservatives." It is between those who are activists and those who are not. History shows us that what tempts justices toward activism is not so much political philosophy as simply being in the majority of the Court. Control of

83

the Court, from either political direction, breeds activism. Will conservatives continue to believe in self-restraint if they achieve a solid majority on the court? Justices do not like to make law—until they can. When they have five sure votes, they tend to run with the ball.

There are exceptions, of course. Frankfurter fell from fashion because he was consistent. But such consistency is rare, since it tends to vanish once the Outs become the Ins. Liberals are more blatant about activism, but conservatives on the Court, whether William Howard Taft or William H. Rehnquist, have proven just as capable of getting the job done.

Rule by the courts is arguably the most burdensome legacy of the New Elite, and its impact may be even more pronounced in the future. As those of one political philosophy or another seek to write their own notions into law, with no restraint from themselves or the public, the immigrant wisdom of Justice Frankfurter may be recognized at last for what it really is: a timeless warning that if consent of the governed is not our goal, it will become our memory.

PART TWO

The Way We Live Now

SIX

Test Scores Up, Culture Down

The New Elite has transformed our culture as much as it has our politics. Everyone decries the erosion of values in popular culture. Movies stink. Most books and magazines stink. Television really stinks. The golden age of popular culture has been displaced by "reality" shows, scatological commercials, and "accidental" nudity. There is wide agreement that most popular culture now is clearly aimed at the lowest common denominator.

But why? In, say, the 1930s, movies, the stage, literature, and all the other popular arts seemed to reach for a higher level, both morally and intellectually, than is the case now. But then, a great deal of this popular culture was created by immigrants or the children of immigrants, who often had very little education. Today, those who control movie studios, television networks, and so on tend to be well educated. Frequently, they have M.B.A.s. So why, when the testable ability of the culture purveyors has gone up, has the quality gone down? Because the New Elite has contempt for the audience. The old movie moguls worshipped the audience, from which they themselves had emerged.

And, of course, in those days there was a single audience. It included everyone. There were a few people who never went to movies, but they were a relative handful, a very tiny island in a vast global sea. Most people went to the movies, and often. Most of them were in roughly similar economic circumstances, neither affluent nor starving. They worked very hard. Few attended college. Some were very smart and some were not; most were somewhere in between. Natural ability was far less related to economic status than is the case today. Equality of opportunity was in its infancy. And so the audience—the public, as it then truly could be called—reflected the whole human condition and a considerably shared experience. The most gifted and perceptive members of the audience were unrecognized as such by society, and sometimes even by themselves; you reached them by addressing the audience as a whole.

The moguls believed in the wisdom of the audience. It was hard to dispute the judgment of those who bought one's product so willingly. More important, the moguls knew the audience. They were people like themselves. They were the people they had grown up with, and lived with, until destiny and Edison found a use for celluloid. In a very real sense, sometimes literally, the moguls were making movies for their own families.

All this has changed. Movies are still made by moguls—now known as executives. Some of them started in the mailroom or some other humble studio job. A few are high school dropouts. But today the vast majority of top executives in Hollywood, like their counterparts in every other industry, are very well educated at very good colleges. Their upbringings were entirely different from those of the first movie moguls. Most lived in comfortable neighborhoods and grew up with other children often as bright as themselves. Their universe, though pleasant, was narrow and unvaried. Like the original moguls, they reached a position where they could choose which movies were made for the public, but unlike those moguls, they didn't quite know what the public was. It was an abstraction. They were not making movies for their own families, or for themselves. Instead, when anticipating the audience for their work, "they assume a hollowed-eyed, empty-souled, know-nothing hick."

This quote is from a genuine cultural icon, the late great film critic Pauline Kael, who was writing in *The New Yorker* on August 5, 1974. In the same essay, she also says,

> Perhaps no work of art is possible without belief in the audience—the kind of belief that has nothing to do with facts and figures about what people actually buy or enjoy but comes out of the individual artist's absolute conviction that only the best he can do is fit to be offered to others. It's what makes a director insist on a retake even when he knows he's going to be penalized for it; it's what makes young dancers drop from exhaustion; it's what made Caruso burst his throat. You have to believe in the audience, and believe that your peak effort just barely makes you worthy of it. That's implicit when an artist says he does it "because he has to," and even when he says he did it "just for himself." An artist's sense of honor is founded on the honor due others. Honor in the arts—and in show business, too—is giving of one's utmost, even if the audience does not appear to know the difference, even if the audience shows every sign of preferring something easy, cheap, and synthetic. The audience one must believe in is the great audience, the audience one was part of as a child, when one first began to respond to great work—the audience one

is still a part of. As soon as an artist ceases to see himself as part of the audience—when he begins to believe that what matters is to satisfy the jerk audience out there—he stops being an artist.

Well, the first moguls were seldom artists, but they did believe passionately that their audiences were worthy of their highest achievements, and so art often did occur within their studios. Just read the accounts of the making of *Casablanca,* of the extraordinary involvement of the producer and of the head of the studio, Jack Warner, in their endless efforts to improve each scene, each line of dialogue. There was more than the lure of profit to such obsessive dedication—theirs was a frenzied zeal to make the movie better, and no one has said as well as Pauline Kael why it had to be better, and for whom.

Yes, many duds were turned out by those studios, but *Casablanca* isn't the exception, it's the rule: that popular culture can be sublime when there's respect for the mass audience.

There are so many examples of this. When Evelyn Waugh visited Hollywood, he was introduced to Charlie Chaplin and Walt Disney. Having met the only two geniuses the place had produced, he said, he was free to return to England. If ever two filmmakers were engaged in reaching a mass audience, it was these two, whose gifts Waugh correctly defined.

Of course, there were more than two. John Ford made westerns. Alfred Hitchcock made suspense films. And today they're seen as among the very greatest artists in the history of the medium. The "art" that was self-consciously attempted by the Golden Age moguls has fared less well—Norma Shearer and Leslie Howard as Romeo and Juliet! The audience knew what real art was, and they flocked to *Stagecoach* and *Notorious.* Who would have guessed in the 1930s that the Marx fated to be worshipped on our campuses would be Groucho, not Karl?

Today's executives, for the most part, do not believe in the audience. For them, it is not "the audience one was part of as a child." They were never part of the great audience of everyone. Today's executives can feel exaltation only in the smaller audiences of those quite like themselves. They know that's not a large enough audience to make "art" profitable. And they no longer think (because they don't know people in that audience) that the great audience can appreciate anything good. And, since they do very much want to make money, they therefore "assume a hollow-eyed, empty-souled, know-nothing hick."

This is why so many movies are so bad today. And movies are only one example. In all the arts and in mass entertainment, the quality plummets as those in charge of output become increasingly members of the new IQ class. One might think that a truly new elite would improve the level of our general culture. Instead, it is destroying it. It is destroying it through contempt for the general audience.

Such contempt is nothing new. Many screenwriters in the 1930s (though seldom the best) had contempt for the audience, too, and often expressed it. But they weren't in charge of making films. Or, very often, in charge of publishing houses, art galleries, or theaters. Now they are. A new class is in charge of the distribution of art, and it has no reverence for the audience. Almost no one who does revere the audience is allowed to reach it. The frustration of real artists is shared by the great audience, which has contempt for the junk it is offered.

Just because the New Elite is certain that the majority is incapable of enjoying great art does not mean that the new class enjoys that capability itself. The lives of most members of the new class seem sadly remote from culture or beauty. They sneer at the junk movies and junk books that they themselves consign to the masses, but what do they see, what do they read? The *Macbeth* they bought at the college co-op is valueless to them now: dusty, brittle pages never reread since it was first assigned. The new class interest in great literature seems to be highly related to what public television imports from England. Dramatizations probably are better than nothing, and they are certainly superior to what the new class actually reads: self-improvement or New Age pap, or novels without structure or values.

In any event, most members of the New Elite read very little. They simply don't have the time. A meritocracy by definition is very hardworking. Increasingly, both spouses have demanding jobs. At the end of each grueling day, they spend most of their few remaining waking hours chauffeuring children between athletic events or maintaining and supplying their homes.

For it is a virtually servantless class. It is more fortunate than most—nannies are not uncommon—but it is still part of its age, and in the age of equality of opportunity domestic help was the first luxury to go. Many who polished and cleaned and ironed and shopped in the recent past were at least as able as their employers. If they wielded mops rather than gavels, it was because there was little social or economic mobility. But now merit is rewarded. The granddaughter of a maid may be a judge. But she will not have a maid. In offices and factories, the pay is almost certain to be higher than in domestic service.

Few today are clamoring to work as servants. Even the very rich get along with far less help than their grandparents considered minimal. And those in the new class—comfortable but seldom wealthy—generally have no live-in help at all. And as a consequence, they have no leisure, either. For the first time in history, educated people work longer hours than those without diplomas. They return each evening to servantless homes and fierce domestic agendas.

The result is an absence of leisure. And leisure is a prerequisite of culture. Not just the creation of culture, but its appreciation as well. The production of thought and beauty is advanced by an audience able to evaluate and judge and compare, an audience informed and alert and engaged.

That audience is almost extinct. It persists in enclaves on some campuses, and there are stubborn pockets of it elsewhere. But there is no longer a pervasive leisured class whose members know by rote the old poets and so are able to debate the merits of the new. There were probably more members of this leisured class in the bad old days, when fewer than 5 percent of the population sought higher education, than now, when the number is close to half.

Nor is leisure the only factor. Even more important is the growth of specialization in the workplace, and therefore in higher education as well. Many more people are highly educated today than previously, but they are often more narrowly educated. Everyone needs to specialize. A Ph.D. in Asian studies shows not the least interest on being told that it was not in fact, as she had stated, Shakespeare who wrote the line "April is the cruelest month," because, after all, "that's not my field." Once the educated wandered through many fields. A college education, formerly thought to be an end in itself, is today just a ticket to a graduate school.

The ticket to college itself is the Scholastic Aptitude Test, which tests ability, not knowledge. The author of the SAT, Carl Brigham, did not design it for the purpose of sifting college applicants. In fact, when such usage was proposed in 1938, he fired off an angry letter to President James Bryant Conant of Harvard. That letter was, alas, quite prescient. It says in part:

> If the unhappy day ever comes when teachers point their students toward these newer examinations, . . . then we may look for the inevitable distortion of education in terms of tests. And that means that mathematics will continue to be completely departmentalized and broken into disintegrated bits, that the sciences will become highly verbalized and that computation, manipulations and thinking in terms other than verbal will be minimized, that languages will be taught for linguistic skills only without reference to literacy values, that English will be taught for reading alone, and that practice and drill in the writing of English will disappear. (As quoted in Nicholas Lemann, *The Big Test*, 40–41)

This warning, however dire, was understated. It is possible today—indeed, it is common—for a young person to graduate from an elite preparatory school, then an elite college, and then an elite law school, and even after that final matriculation not be able to compose an essay in cogent or stirring prose. One is speaking here not of the absence of style, but of the lack of lucidity itself, the incapacity to deploy words tactically across the plane of reason in order to embrace, convert, or demolish another point of view—to fan the coals for warmth and flame.

The same person could write well had that ever been demanded, in classroom exercises or as a prerequisite to the ascending levels of education. The natural ability was there—the verbal test score shows it. It's as if once that test score was known, and the superior ability of the student was certified, no use need be made of that ability. Our educational system is increasingly interested in the measurement of "ability" and less and less concerned with accomplishment in life. IQ certification by testing is considered enough, an end in itself, a valid predictor for subsequent performance in similar tests. The test score is not connected with any other intellectual or moral aspect of life, nor does its use acknowledge that such could exist.

No wonder the level of general culture is so low, and falling. Contempt for the audience and isolation from it, the lack of leisure, the ubiquity of specialization, and a system of education that rewards who one is rather than what one does all have left us with a new class, virtually the ruling class in terms of cultural authority, incapable of knowing what is good, let alone best, in the life of the mind or the quest of the soul for beauty.

Culture, like democracy, depends on values as well as intellect. It cannot be nurtured by valueless technocrats. And if these technocrats control the bureaucracies that control the museums and orchestras and publishing, neither art nor entertainment will be nurtured from any other source, for access to the audience is controlled by those who loathe the audience.

Art does need an elite, but of accomplishment, not test scores. Art does need patrons, but those who want to admire, not certify. They need not be specially trained. As it turns out, Pope Julius, the patron of Michelangelo, was a better judge of beauty than a committee of Ph.D.s.

Art is no better certified by committees than by plebiscites. New truths are found and expressed by a few. They are special and rare and brave, and their dreams become the bulwark of our lives. But those dreams are now denied, not by a totalitarian state, but by a new class that professes, and probably believes, that it wants to promote the higher things in life. For this, it is necessary to have some connection with life itself.

SEVEN

Enron and the SAT

As America entered the twenty-first century, it was not only the freest and most powerful nation on earth, it was also by far the richest.

The 1990s had been a period of domestic prosperity unprecedented in human history. There was considerable dispute as to how equitably that wealth was distributed within the nation; but as to the size of the golden egg, there was no question. How could there be? Whether aircraft or fast foods, software or movies with explosions and car chases, America was turning out in astonishing abundance the products that the rest of the world was very anxious to buy.

And a majority of Americans saw their lives improved, perhaps not always in quality but certainly in terms of material possessions and recreational choices that had not been dreamed of by their parents. The rising tide may have lifted yachts higher than dinghies, but secretaries now were no more likely to drink free office coffee than they were to down a glass of tap water— better alternatives were only an elevator ride and five bucks away.

The heroes of this new abundance were the CEOs. Business executives, recalling perhaps the social unrest of the Vietnam years, imagined they were still reviled when in fact in most quarters they had become adored. Worshipped. Acknowledged as the architects of those wonderfully open floodgates. Why else would the public yawn at the fact that a CEO now was paid four hundred times the salary of a worker on the assembly line? Why not? These were the gods who caused a rain of gold. They were the calm, clear, decisive, hardworking entrepreneurs and executives whose rational deliberations had led to such great prosperity. Thanks for the latte, guys, and hope you enjoy your Gulfstream.

Suddenly, this all changed. CEOs were in disgrace. The sight of an executive arriving for his arraignment in Armani and handcuffs was enough to transform the average TV viewer into Madame Defarge. Bring on the tumbrels! More! More!

What had happened began with Enron. Once heralded as one of the largest corporations in the land (even this fact turned out to be a lie), Enron became the symbol of corporate evildoers, executives whose deceit had caused the oversold plane to crash while they themselves escaped in golden parachutes.

The books indeed had been cooked and the executives wildly overcompensated. But, then, these flaws were revealed in other companies—Tyco, for example. More tumbrels *were* needed. Still, Enron remained the symbol for executive perfidy: greed, fraud, self-dealing, vast webs spun of pure deceit, lack of concern or regard for the trusting shareholders.

And so it came about that CEOs lost favor in the public eye. Only a handful of companies were even accused of fraud. Most were honestly managed. But the scandals had heightened a level of suspicion from which, however unfairly, no corporation seemed exempt.

There also was the question of compensation. So long as the stock market was going up, people had ignored the soaring executive salaries. When the market began a huge decline—fueled in part by the perception that even a company as large as Enron could be run by con artists—all that bloated compensation became less tolerable. Even Jack Welch, who had honestly multiplied the shareholders' value in General Electric many times over, became a focal point of public outrage over the perks he received on retirement. If Welch could be vilified—Welch, who had ranked highest in the pantheon of CEOs so widely worshipped—then no CEO was safe. Admiration of business leaders had been transformed into a harsher reaction somewhere between hatred and contempt.

All of the above is well known to the reader. So what does it have to do with the New Elite?

Plenty. Enron's problems, and those of the other misfeasors, would never have occurred had the new class been doing its job. In every field, there are a few crooks and charlatans. So this is true as well of business—most executives are honest and hardworking, but there will always be some who are not. Not many, but enough. Enough to require supervision.

And who are these supervisors? To a significant extent, they are members of the New Elite. Each company is occupied by an army of new class monitors.

Their tasks are clearly defined. Few familiar with large publicly traded companies would claim that they are insufficiently regulated. Such companies must by law provide a vast amount of information to innumerable sharp-eyed professionals, both publicly and privately employed. The SEC alone is a vacuum cleaner continuously on, sucking up incredible quantities of data with which to measure the corporation's compliance with federal regulations.

Then there are lawyers, both in-house and outside the company. Not all represent the company; some are in the service of shareholders or raiders or other companies. These lawyers have varying degrees of access to the company's financial secrets, but to none of them can information be entirely denied.

And of course there are the accountants. Nothing in theory is hidden from them. Their job is to sign off on whether everything is in order. In Enron's case, Arthur Andersen did opine that all was well, and in consequence it soon went out of business. The Big Five accounting firms became the slightly larger Big Four.

Accountants, lawyers, and government regulators were not the only ones who failed to see the massive Enron problems. There were others, too, whose eyeshades were blindfolds: securities analysts, investment bankers, money managers, and all those highly trained specialists who have been certified as able to examine complex financial data and then understand what the numbers really mean.

And beyond (or perhaps above) even all of these is another class of super-consultant, the management-consulting firms. Of these, the largest and most prestigious, the top of the mountain, higher even than the clouds, is the almost reverentially regarded hothouse of ultimate testable ability, the legendary McKinsey & Company.

McKinsey is in the business of hiring the best of the brightest, those intrepid climbers who dwell atop Everest and have nowhere left to look but down. The largest corporations in the land send for help from their base camps; and from on high the most gifted descend to advise, to solve, to awe, to heal, then ascend once more to the lofty peak that lesser mortals will never attain.

In the July 22, 2002, *New Yorker,* Malcolm Gladwell's aptly titled "The Talent Myth: Are Smart People Overrated?" notes that "of all [McKinsey's] clients, one firm took the talent mind-set closest to heart. It was a company where McKinsey conducted twenty separate projects, where McKinsey's billings topped ten million dollars a year, where a McKinsey director regularly attended board meetings, and where the CEO himself was a former McKinsey partner. The company, of course, was Enron. . . ."

"The one Enron partner that has escaped largely unscathed is McKinsey, which is odd, given that it essentially created the blueprint for the Enron culture. Enron was the ultimate 'talent' company. . . . During the nineties, Enron was bringing in two hundred and fifty newly minted M.B.A.'s a year. 'We had these things called Super Saturdays,' one former Enron manager recalls. 'I'd interview some of these guys who were fresh out of Harvard, and these kids could blow me out of the water. They knew things I'd never heard of. . . .

"The management of Enron, in other words, did exactly what the consultants at McKinsey said that companies had to do in order to succeed in the modern economy. It hired and rewarded the very best and the very brightest—and it is now in bankruptcy."

One of the high points of Gladwell's excellent article is his description of an experiment conducted by Carol Dweck, a psychologist at Columbia University. "Dweck gave a class of preadolescent students a test filled with challenging problems. After they were finished, one group was praised for its effort and another group was praised for its intelligence. Those praised for their intelligence were reluctant to tackle difficult tasks, and their performance on subsequent tests soon began to suffer. Then Dweck asked the children to write a letter to students at another school, describing their experience in the study. She discovered something remarkable: forty per cent of those students who were praised for their intelligence lied about how they had scored on the test, adjusting their grade upward. They weren't naturally deceptive people, and they weren't any less intelligent or self-confident than anyone else. *They simply did what people do when they are immersed in an environment that celebrates them solely for their innate 'talent.' They began to define themselves by that description, and when times get tough and that self-image is threatened they have difficulty with the consequences. They will not take the remedial course. They will not stand up to investors and the public and admit that they were wrong. They'd sooner lie"* (emphasis added).

With very few exceptions, brilliant academic stars, particularly the consultants and watchdogs, failed to do their jobs. They failed not because they lacked the technical skills or the structures for supervision. Their failure was moral. The problem was not lack of regulation, but rather the moral vacuity of the regulators.

Put as simply as possible, these superstars cared only about what was legal or illegal, and they never thought about what was right or wrong. Because unless they were lucky in their parentage, no one had ever *taught* them right from wrong. After all, it isn't something you can *quantify*. It isn't something you can *memorize*.

That's because the thing about right and wrong is that the distinction be-tween them is (in their view) *subjective*. An entire generation has been taught to give a pass to subjectivity. They've been trained to suspend judgment. Often they've been told that there *is* no such thing as right or wrong—it's all subjec-tive. Different people have different views, and all supposedly must be re-spected. Respect for other people's views is one thing. Saying that all views are morally equal is another. There *is* such a thing as objective morality, but that's out of fashion now. Instead, students are taught the really frightening doctrine of moral relativism, which has caused them to believe that concepts of right and wrong have little or no meaning.

And there's another characteristic of the New Elite that left all its whis-tles unblown. As we have elsewhere observed, and as the Dweck study con-firms, high on the new class list of commandments is the habitual avoidance of risk. Risk is for the marketplace, and the New Elite hates the marketplace. It rewards people, often richly, who ranked lower academically than you-know-who. Risk brings gains, but it can also bring losses, and the New Elite already has achieved its greatest gain—the jobs and status won by test scores. Its members will progress somewhat higher in their chosen worlds through seniority and expertise, if only they remember not to rock the boat. It is *risky* to be a whistle-blower, and given that you don't believe in right or wrong, what's the point?

It is quite true that not all accountants, lawyers, analysts, and so on are members of the New Elite. If their self-identity is not based on inclusion within a so-called measurably superior class, then they are Left Behinds, how-ever well educated. True, some of these could have blown their whistles, too, and did not, for reasons no worthier than those of their insular peers—greed, complicity, a personal financial stake in the outcome. (Left Behinds, too, are perfectly capable of putting career above principle.)

But it is not unreasonable to assume that most of those who chose to ig-nore the pigs at the trough were unabashed members of the New Elite. They almost had to be. Virtually all of them owed their jobs to test scores: on the SAT, the LSAT, the Series Seven, and every other test that ranks the scores of those who take it. Summa or magna, these people had been *certified* as the best and the brightest. And because of their scores, they had been rewarded, put in charge of watching a huge and fabled company, Enron. And they did watch it. In fact, watching was all they did.

And they didn't even do that well. Not only did they speak no evil, they didn't seem to see or hear it, either. If it couldn't be quantified, fuggedaboutit!

Put another way, they thought that being *rational* was enough. But cogitation without morality is not rational. What thousands of professionals, all of whom had been classroom stars, were doing was divorced from a moral framework, walled off from experience, oblivious to human nature, insulated totally from everything that cannot be numerically tested.

But various educators and college admissions officers are indignant at such charges. *Of course* they think morality is important. They *demand* it of students. But what they really demand is *evidence* of morality. Quantitative evidence: How many hours per week did you spend helping those less fortunate than yourself? Everybody who answers this question turns out to be very, very moral. High schools, with an eye to college admissions officers, *require* a certain number of hours of worthy work among the needy, and the students, with the same but far more zealous competitive motive, serve coffee in the old folks' home (though many wouldn't think of phoning their own grandparents—you don't get admissions points for that, and anyway there's always a big exam to study for). Presumably, some of those who overlooked Enron's failings had also accumulated a zillion hours of well-documented community service. And had written essays in which they declared their role model to be Mother Teresa. They were just doing what they've always done: competing.

But even so, one might say, the rules that were broken were in writing. There were *laws,* in black and white. The SEC rules against fraud are manifold and clear. How could the watchdogs have missed a violation of law? The answer, alas, is that when you think that there is no such thing as right or wrong, only what is legal or illegal, then any bending or pressing or convolution of language that outrageously but technically casts what is being done as legal, or as the watchdogs obviously prefer, not absolutely, positively illegal, will do.

And you think *that* convoluted sentence is an exaggeration? Well, here's another, more simply stated: When a married member of the New Elite is accused of having had sex with a very young woman in his employment, and publicly denies the charge, saying "I never had sex with that woman," he very probably thinks he isn't lying because he defines sex as intercourse and they were doing something else. (Not something else that one would casually mention to one's spouse, mind you, because human survival instinct is almost always superior to highly tortured ratiocination; but for public consumption, the technically arguable but absolutely absurd is good enough.)

Though reluctant once again to pick on the same unnamed president (but unable to resist such a treasure trove of examples), let it be said that if you're in and of the New Elite and questioned about sexual misconduct, you think that there's nothing wrong with saying, "That depends on what the meaning of 'is' is." How can these people say these things? No one, not even they, would say such things to their spouses. Who, then, are they speaking to? Do they think that those outside their circle are idiots? Or do they believe that such fraudulently nuanced interpretation is the same thing as, or even close to, truth? Who knows? But we do know what people publicly say

This is not a failing only of presidents. It is a failing of a class—to which at least one president arguably belongs.

So, once again, what happened with Enron? What happened is that you can't test virtue.

But you can teach it. At least you can try. If not in the classroom, at least in the home, and surely by public example. Reasonable people sometimes will differ over what is right and what is wrong, but surely they should be informed that there are such concepts as right and wrong, and that just because something might be arguably legal doesn't mean it should be done. We can't have a law for every problem, but we can have a moral code that covers all problems.

The above applies as well to wildly excessive executive compensation, but here the New Elite is not directly to blame. The compensation in virtually every case was undeniably legal. And those who voted for it were corporate board members, few of whom are members of the New Elite. Virtually none of the executives who received (indeed, engineered) this gross largesse were members of it, either. All of these people put more faith in the efficacy of the marketplace than in the ratiocinations of experts, so they're squarely in the camp of the Left Behinds.

But their actions have to some extent been influenced by the new class they despise. The loss of belief in nonquantifiable standards has seeped into the national culture. Even businessmen who in every other way are antithetical to the New Elite are not immune from the recent pollution of standards, the subtle retreat from the concept of right versus wrong. So if they can get massive bonuses while the company's stock is sinking, why not? Greed becomes habitual when there is no one around to object.

But what about the stockholders? Why have they been so silent? One reason is that much of the stock is owned by huge institutions and funds. Those who run those funds follow each corporation carefully, but they really don't seem to care about executive compensation. It's legal and it's such a small percentage of the corporation's total wealth—isn't it? The supposedly rational thing, then, is to turn away from such a subjective question as whether such compensation is *unfair.*

Wildly excessive executive compensation is relatively new. In the not so olden days, executives were paid ten or perhaps twenty times as much as their lowest-paid employees. (We are speaking of salaried compensation, including stock options, not wealth from ownership.) They didn't get more because they never dared to ask for more, and had they asked for more, the board would have been reluctant to comply. So would the shareholders, who in many cases were members of the family that started the business. Most executives, board members, and stockholders (the shareholder class was formerly much smaller than now) believed in a moral code, however imperfectly some practiced it. Those who ran companies were often highly intelligent, but they put their greatest emphasis not on academic achievement but on character. It was a world in which a handshake was worth more than a hundred signed documents. These values are still reflected in many businesses, large and small.

Yes, it's better now that corporate hiring is no longer restricted by social, gender, and racial considerations. It's good as well that people who have done well in school should be rewarded. What is not good is the increasing absence of moral standards. Moral relativism permitted very smart people to overlook very bad things. We must be careful not to impose our moral views on others, but we should stop assuming, and sometimes promoting, that whatever works for you is great. There is a higher standard.

There is no SAT test for predicting good citizenship—there never can or should be. You can't quantitatively test character and decency. The most effective way to serve your community is consistently to do the right thing for the right reason. Whatever we're testing our brightest students for now, we're not producing enough good citizens—or even enough who care to be. We don't need to change the tests. We surely need to raise our values.

EIGHT

The Rise of the SATocracy

In London in 1950, a very dull meeting was drawing to a close. Most of the observers were technical staff, but despite their supposed interest in the subject under discussion, some were clearly nodding. Not Michael Young, though. His eyes were alert as he watched the proceedings. He was a brilliant sociologist and an adviser to the Labour Party. The meeting that transfixed him was of the National Joint Council for Industry. But it wasn't the data that held his attention. It was the people.

For it was a meeting of the leaders of two different worlds—industry and labor. Two different worlds and two different upbringings— one of the utmost privilege, the other of stark denial. The difference was greatest, perhaps, in terms of the education that each group had received. The captains of industry had attended the most elite schools. Many of the union representatives had scarcely been educated at all—harsh necessity had driven them to full-time labor at a very early age. It was the knowledge of this disparity that fascinated Michael Young. Because as he watched the two groups in action, debating and maneuvering against each other, one question was paramount in his mind: "Did any group have more ability than another?"

He was later to elaborate on this question, and to answer it: "Were the trade unionists outmanoeuvered in argument because they left school at thirteen or fourteen while the leaders of private industry had been to Cambridge? . . . Were the trade union leaders at a disadvantage because they were shoved into a factory at an age when the others were still in short trousers? Obviously not—if anything the advantage was the other way round. The trade unionists not only spoke from longer experience. They included some of the ablest men in the country."

Young saw how very bright they were—for they had been raised at a time when even a genius, if born in a colliery village, would likely spend his life in the mines. But Young saw something else as well. He knew the labor leaders. He had worked closely with them, and he saw that their children were not being raised as they themselves had been. No coal mines for them. If not actually Eton, their schools were very good. The offspring of these brilliant if uneducated labor leaders might not be quite as brilliant themselves, but they were certainly going to be well educated. They would not be laborers. They would be doctors or lawyers or whatever else was compatible with their ability and their education.

For the world was changing. After World War II, in some of the more advanced countries, equality of opportunity was becoming truly widespread for the first time, the rule rather than the exception. In some cases, doors were still closed to the able—most blacks in America, for example—but as a general rule, and on a scale unprecedented in history, children could aspire to and achieve careers that reflected and utilized their full ability. This trend was widely applauded by almost everyone Michael Young knew, and certainly by all the laborers with whom his work brought him in contact. To them, equality of opportunity seemed a dream come true. It meant everyone could rise to his or her own level.

But Young saw farther. He saw that it meant the creation of a new class: an IQ class. He saw the transformation of society, with new stratification even more rigid than the class lines of the past. He decided to write a book about what he saw coming. His first problem was what to call this new class. "The IQ Class" lacked elegance. Finally, Young decided to invent a name. His brave new word was "meritocracy." It was a combination of Latin and Greek, and no one had ever seen it before. While nowadays everyone uses the word, most are unaware of its fairly recent origin.

Young's book is called *The Rise of the Meritocracy,* and it is a work of satire. Published in 1958, his account takes place far in an imagined future, in the year 2034. It is written in the form of an essay by someone named Michael Young (apparently one creative new name per book was enough), a scholar with special expertise in the long-departed days of the twentieth century.

This essayist of 2034 is a product of the meritocracy and endorses the new order completely. With a certain amount of smugness (and a literary style of exceptional lucidity), he describes his near-perfect world. It is a world in which one's station in life is determined entirely by measured IQ. Tests for the measurement of intelligence have become progressively more reliable, and so in 2034 it is now possible to ascertain with total accuracy the IQ of a three-year-old. This makes education so much more efficient. The very brightest children are sent to one kind of school, the less bright to other kinds of schools. There they are trained for their proper roles in life. Those with the highest IQs will hold the highest posts. The less gifted will be laborers; but to avoid the shame attached to such a classification, they will be known as "technicians." There is total equality of opportunity. Every high-IQ person has been identified and rewarded with a high job. No longer must a genius waste his life in a coal mine.

So when the National Joint Council meets in 2034, with management on one side of the table and labor on the other, one need no longer be dismayed at ability unrelated to station. That has all been fixed. No longer is talent randomly scattered around the table. "On the one side sit the IQs of 140, on the other the IQs of 99." Equality of opportunity has reached its logical conclusion.

In such a world, all you need to know about a person is his or her IQ. It is highlighted in each entry in *Who's Who*. Each person carries a National Intelligence Card, which reveals not only one's identity but by implication one's social and economic class, because "by imperceptible degrees an aristocracy of birth has turned into an aristocracy of talent." Indeed, "Now that people are classified by ability, the gap between the classes has inevitably become wider."

Of course, the new order attempts to be fair. Those who think that they're smarter than their IQ scores can always retake the test. But once the score is finally known, it determines everything.

Though written as satire, Young's book is astonishingly prophetic. Quite apart from the central prediction, the stratification of society by IQ, Young is prescient in a host of imagined particulars that follow. He saw not only the growth of a new tree, but also the fruit that it would bear. He saw that young people would increasingly occupy the highest positions, and he anticipated the growth of feminism. These offshoots were the inevitable (and happy) result of emphasizing merit over everything else, including gender and experience.

Young saw as well what he called "the new unemployment," by which he meant the highly selective unemployment that is apparent today. While the high-IQ class will be very busy indeed, the lower-rung jobs will be increasingly displaced by machines. Young saw that many stores would be largely self-service, an amazing insight for his own time and place. He also anticipated the astonishing segregation, in classroom, workplace, and neighborhood, of the new classes.

And he saw something else, too, ominous in its portent. He saw that the new class would want to be permanent. It would want its status to be hereditary. In the book, when two bright parents have a child significantly less bright, they are supposed to accept the fact that the child's life will have less status and comfort than their own. But they do not accept it. Parents are parents, and they refuse to consign their children to a life less rich than their own.

So some come up with schemes to avoid such a fate. They insist, for example, that the less bright children of high-IQ parents be given an elite education anyway. After all, "most of them will not be all that less intelligent than their parents; but the polish given them in their homes will fit them to succeed to the élite. . . . [A]ny loss of effectiveness in the meritocracy will be more than outweighed by the benefits of making it hereditary. Parents will be easier on their minds and their children will not have to go through all the psychological stresses of having to prove themselves in competition with children from the lower classes. . . . [T]he body politic will gain in stability."

Still other privileged parents are intrigued by new experiments suggesting "controlled mutations in the genetic constitutions of the unborn can be induced by means of radiation so as to raise the level of intelligence above that which would otherwise be yielded." Should such experiments prove successful, "the crucial question would be, whose children are to have their intelligence artificially raised in this manner?" To which the fictional Young answers, "Obviously the decision must rest with the meritocracy, not the democracy who have no means of weighing the gravity of the issue." (Will this be the case when DNA tampering is even more effective than "radiation"?) In the meantime, other upper-class parents advocate laws permitting only themselves to adopt high-IQ babies from the lower classes.

For some reason, parents in the other classes do not take kindly to these trends. Not to worry, says the author. "The lower classes no longer have the power to make revolt effective." Young is certain that the dissidents will be easily overcome at the great meeting on the subject scheduled for May at Peterloo.

And that is the end of the book—except for this footnote:

> 1. Since the author of this essay was himself killed at Peterloo, the publishers regret that they were not able to submit to him the proofs of his manuscript. . . . The text, even this last section, has been left exactly as he wrote it. The failings of sociology are as illuminating as its successes.

The Rise of the Meritocracy caused quite a stir. It made many readers very angry. Some even thought that the future (fictional) Michael Young was the same man as the actual author of the satire and believed the same things. They couldn't understand that Young was predicting what he thought was going to happen, not necessarily what he wanted to occur.

Many of his predictions have already proven all too accurate. Though not in every case. But even when he is wrong, his misses are as instructive as his bull's-eyes in helping us understand the new class. Some of his mistakes are merely amusing, such as Young's prediction that there would be a vast increase in the number of domestic servants. Since the lower-IQ people would have trouble finding jobs, and the higher-IQ class would need to devote most of its time to its important work, it seemed to Young that one class would end up keeping house for the other. (This, as any harassed two-lawyer couple today can testify, has not proven to be the case.) Equally off the mark is Young's prediction that the new lower classes would occupy much of their time in physical fitness programs; as it turned out, members of the New Elite are far likelier to spend time on Stairmasters, with the Left Behinds content to be couch potatoes. But these are details. The great gulf between Young's imagined world and our own is in the area of education. And the disparity is startling.

It helps to understand the world at the time of the real Michael Young. All students in Britain, on completing elementary school, were given the "11-plus" exam, the results of which affected the rest of their lives. Those whose scores were in the top 20 percent were allowed to attend state "grammar schools," which prepared them for a university. The rest received a vocational education, which ended when they were fifteen. Originally, the 11-plus exam had an IQ section that, though repealed later on, was very much in effect when Young wrote his book.

Young's meritocracy flowers first and foremost in Britain, because its system of education is primed to nurture it. Teachers (of the high-IQ students) are paid well enough to compete with private industry for the best scientists. In his view, real meritocracy could not occur in the United States because the people there demanded "comprehensive" schools—children of all abilities attended the same school, with no separate education for the gifted.

But it certainly did not turn out that way. Today, the growth and success of a new IQ elite seem more evident in the United States than in Britain. Young was correct in seeing that America would insist on "comprehensive" schools. Yet despite the persistence of supposedly equalitarian public education, a vast number of high-IQ students in the United States are identified early on and educated in a manner appropriate to their abilities. How can this be?

Because, truth be told, we do not in fact have "comprehensive" education. We pay lip service to something that has long since ceased to exist. Young is quite correct that an IQ elite cannot exist without an educational system that finds and nurtures it. And that is exactly what we now have in the United States—for a great many children—despite all the school board protestations to the contrary.

It happened in two ways. First, a significant number of high-IQ students do not attend public schools. The doctor and the lawyer who are married to one another may not be millionaires, but they are often able to send their children to private schools. Even if such education represents a real financial sacrifice, it is increasingly chosen by well-educated parents because a good education is their highest priority, and the decline of public schools in many areas has made the private alternative far more attractive.

Which brings us to the second way that Young's view of American education has proven false—in the nature of our public schools. He saw these as being geared to the lowest common denominator, guaranteeing mediocrity rather than promoting meritocracy. What he did not foresee was the wide variety of public schools and the stunning disparity in how they are funded. The districts that need the money the most generally get the least and are vastly outspent by the wealthier suburbs. Some suburban public schools are in effect elite college preparatory institutions. And this is not merely because of superior funding. Not only the very wealthiest can choose where they want to live. There are suburbs for the rich and for the poor and for every gradation in between, social as well as economic. It is not uncommon for vast numbers of professional couples to move to a particular suburb. When the bright children of these bright parents do well, the local school achieves a good reputation, and even more of the same kind of parents start moving in. Consequently, the lowest common denominator can be quite high.[1]

However, there is an even more significant factor at work, and it applies to many public schools, everywhere, not merely those in the more fortunate suburbs. This is known, and not very descriptively, as tracking. "Tracking" refers to different programs for different students within the same school. The brightest students are in one room, and the others are across the hall (or on different floors). In America, merit is sought out and tested and rewarded with an education different from what other students get. We just don't talk about it. Once again, it is not bad that merit is rewarded. It is a positive good that a poor child with a high IQ can be found and helped to lead the richest and most useful life possible. But to think that a meritocracy is not arising because our schools are "comprehensive" is quite mistaken.

So it is America, not Britain, in which the new class has most obviously flourished. While the United States never has had an 11-plus exam, it does have two-track schools and shocking variance in the quality of its schools. And all these disparate streams of primary and secondary education flow toward a common dam in which the sluice gates are opened only to some, in which the fraudulence of "comprehensive" opportunity is revealed.

Our sluice now is the SAT. There are other things of course—grades, class rank, the quality of the schools in which the grades and class rank are attained, geography, athletic prowess (a surprisingly big exception to academic criteria). All these things matter—but there is no symbol of selection more dramatic than the SAT. Everyone in the eleventh grade who wants to go to college takes the same test (or the ACT) everywhere in the land.

If Young had been an American, and writing thirty years later, he might have coined another word. A better word, because "meritocracy" suggests that there is such a thing as merit (true), that it varies in people (true), *and that it can be accurately tested* (untrue). The New Elite believes that the test score *is* the merit, so this phenomenon deserves another word: SATocracy.

Young's book may have been off in a few details, but as general prediction it was superb. Equality of opportunity has led to new class stratification. This doesn't mean that he—or we—should be opposed to upward mobility. If anything, we must work to achieve even more equality of opportunity, as it still is denied to some people. But we should also know what this worthy goal will bring.

Our SATocracy is bringing about a new class structure. What it means depends on many things, contingent upon our level of awareness. But one of the things it has meant so far—and this is the central thesis of this book—is that the new educated class no longer believes in majority rule. Consciously or not, the New Elite has in myriad ways, by changes in rules and attitudes, already undermined and dismantled the structure of our democracy. The belief in and the capacity for self-governance daily become more eroded.

Young's book is concerned primarily with the emergence of the new class, not with its political impact. He assumes that the meritocracy will have great political power, but he does not describe the unraveling of the fabric of majority rule as such. This is understandable, as the Britain of Young's time may have been a democracy, but the role of the populace, the power of the majority, was much less pronounced than in the United States. A virtually permanent civil service wielded enormous power with a minimum of accountability. To choose its members by competitive examination, to replace the younger sons of Dukes with the brighter sons of clerks, does not, on the surface, seem very threatening to the principle of majority rule. And while Britain has general elections, they are quite different from those in the United

States; in a parliamentary district, the majority vote decides the winner, but it is, and was during Young's time, the national political party that chooses the candidates, assigning its favorites to safe districts, regardless of where they actually lived.

Even more to the point, in Young's time class stratification was vastly more a part of life in Britain than in the United States. Not that the United States was classless, or that privileged birth was irrelevant; but in Britain, the dominance of a privileged and hereditary elite was both obvious and entrenched. It is understandable that Young should write of the displacement of an old aristocracy by a new one.

However, in America, what is being displaced is the institutionalized tradition of majority rule. It is one thing to say that the finance minister should be bright rather than patrician. It is quite another to believe that the Finance Ministry knows better than the people themselves what the government's priorities should be. Young didn't write more about the threat to majority rule because, in his world, there was less majority rule to be threatened.

A new edition of *The Rise of the Meritocracy* was published in 1994. It contains a new introduction by the then old Young, who died soon after the edition was published. (Incidentally, if one needs additional proof that life exceeds art, Michael Young, the brilliant Labour Party adviser who in 1958 predicted a new aristocracy, had become Lord Young of Dartington.) The introduction to the new edition is most instructive, for Lord Young makes it clear that his book was satire: he was never trying to promote an all-powerful meritocracy. In fact, "if the book is not seen to be counterargument as well as argument, the point of it (or at least a good half point) will be lost."

He goes on to say that "even if it could be demonstrated that ordinary people had less native ability than those selected for high position, that would not mean that they deserved to get less. Being a member of the 'lucky sperm club' confers no moral right to advantage. What one is born with, or without, is not of one's own doing." This last paragraph is critical. Lord Young, who apparently was kind as well as brilliant, does not want those who lack high IQs to suffer from low self-esteem. He may even—it is part of his book—prefer a world in which every person, regardless of station, is paid the same.

But does he believe that the people should govern? We can't really tell. It's one thing to say that all people should be treated the same, or even paid the same. It is another thing entirely to say they each should have the same vote, the same voice, in our society. This is the critical question, and Young's answer isn't clear. One of his counterarguments (against the meritocracy) is expressed in the "Chelsea Manifesto," issued by the Technicians (Workers) Party, a group that wants "every man to be respected for the good that is in him." Accordingly, the goal of the manifesto is a classless society:

> The classless society would be one which both possessed and acted upon plural values. Were we to evaluate people, not only according to their intelligence and their education, their occupation, and their power, but according to their kindliness and their courage, their imagination and sensitivity, their sympathy and generosity, there could be no classes. Who would be able to say that the scientist was superior to the porter with admirable qualities as a father, the civil servant with unusual skill at gaining prizes superior to the lorry-driver with unusual skill at growing roses?

Intentional or not, this expression of a "classless society" is very misleading. While seeming to proclaim that all people are created equal, it does not really deal with democracy. It says that it's just as good to raise roses as to win scholarships, but it doesn't go on from there. It talks about essential worth, but not about political rights. The omissions are patronizing. The erasure of political rights is what the new class is most about, but Young fails to address it. His counterargument, a classless society, is too limited. And we're not going to have a classless society. Yes, we should indeed treat everyone with equal decency, but we are and will remain a society of very disparate skills, needs, and rewards. It is not enough to say that virtue can be found in every class; we must also insist that political judgment is found in every class. No matter how stratified a society may be, the majority of its citizens should make the big political decisions.

In past centuries, many societies proclaimed that the good father was equal in God's eyes to the good scientist—or the brave knight, or whoever else was valued at the time. Jefferson saw the humanity of his slaves, but they remained slaves; he did not follow through with political rights. But the good father is not only as good as the good scientist—he may also be just as smart, at least in making decisions about his own political destiny. In terms of making political decisions, some people may be smarter than others. We just don't know who they are. Measured IQ is irrelevant—it's no trick to find hundreds of brilliant people with opposing political views. But there's no way to quantify or prove what are the answers to the big political questions. Majority rule blends human need, public acceptance, and political legitimacy more often than any theorem could ensure. While minority rights must have absolute protection, this isn't an exception to majority rule: it's the corollary.

The reason we must ask everyone's opinion—the rose grower as well as the academic prizewinner—is not to be nice, but to be right. It's our best hope of finding the right answers to society's questions.

A meritocracy in which everyone is loved but only some get to rule is a very bad substitute for what we should really seek. Many members of the New Elite are quick to say (and think they mean) that every individual is equally worthy of respect. In fact, one of the hallmarks of the New Elite is incessant talk about individual rights. How wonderful if this represented a genuine belief in the worth of each individual. If every individual has an absolute right to everything, then the concept of group rights, of majority rule, becomes meaningless. Perhaps this explains the new class love of "individual rights." Individual rights are important and must be safeguarded; but to really believe in the worth of the individual, one must respect (and permit) that individual's vote.

No matter how much they may praise individual rights, members of the New Elite strongly oppose the most fundamental individual right of all: the right to choose how one is governed. There can be no honest belief in individual rights from those who believe that they alone know best and therefore must decide what is best for everyone else.

The Rise of the Meritocracy is a remarkable book, brilliantly written and all too prescient. While its omissions are understandable, we must ensure they are not our omissions, too. If a "meritocracy" is inevitable, its political outcome is not, so long as we are vigilant about maintaining the structure and goals of our democracy.

In the long run, the people know better than the experts what will best serve their interests. It is possible that the most brilliant assemblage of political thinkers in world history was the group assembled in Philadelphia to write our federal constitution. Yet even they left out the Bill of Rights. It was only when the draft constitution was sent to the states for ratification that those extraordinary guarantees, the real glory of our governance, were added on. Freedom of speech, the separation of church and state, the due process clause—these were amendments. This should serve to remind us that not even geniuses, not even the greatest geniuses, together, miraculously, in the same room and working side by side, can get it absolutely right the first time.

On the big questions, the people know best. Of course, the passengers can't take turns steering the ship, but at least they should be able to choose its direction. And, on occasion, elect a new captain. True, people on one side of the bargaining table may be brighter than those on the other. We may have separated out the ablest in science and in some other fields of human endeavor. But not when it comes to elections. There's no way to rank people in a polling booth; it would be folly to try. It's better just to count the votes, and to remember E. B. White's definition: "Democracy is the sneaking suspicion that more than half the people are right more than half of the time."

NOTE

1. We are accustomed to viewing demographic maps that break down large metropolitan areas into their component parts and identify particular characteristics. For example, a map of, say, Chicago and its suburbs may be designed to show the disparity of incomes. This would be illustrated by the use of color—red for wards where the income is under $20,000, yellow for $20,000 to $30,000, and so on. We see such descriptive maps all the time—for income, for ethnic breakdown, for family size, for average age. We do not see such maps depicting the IQ of each neighborhood or suburb, because there is no way at present to obtain that information. But if we had it, and a map were drawn, the patchwork quilt would be as variegated as that for any other category. In some instances, the political line demarcating one suburb from another might separate an average IQ spread of more than twenty points. This is speculative, of course, but it is surely consistent with observable trends. There is a clear correlation between IQ and education, and between education and income. And people of similar incomes and values tend to live near one another. Of course, the correlation is still quite imperfect; there are geniuses in inner-city slums and morons in affluent suburbs. But the trend is clear.

NINE

The Collapse of Moral Relativism

Different times have different needs. Different times breed different heroes.
Now, for the first time in four decades, firefighters and police are being ac-
corded the same respect as law clerks. And the sense of oneness in the nation
has been much restored, allowing us to see America as a community, a community as diverse as the victims of the World Trade Center.

One prays that this retreat from a new class structure will continue,
though the odds are against it. But the ghastly attack on America on September 11, 2001, produced two legacies that may well endure and help to mend
our social fabric. The first is philosophical, the other political.

The philosophical change is the more important. It is the collapse of the
pernicious doctrine known as moral relativism.

This was the moral code of the New Elite. Or rather, it was the *lack* of a
moral code within the New Elite. It's disbelief posing as belief. It's the absolute certainty that there are no absolutes. It's the insistence that there is no
such thing as right or wrong.

You have no choice but to believe this if you don't believe in the wisdom
of the majority.

It works like this: the New Elite uses morality as an excuse to prevail despite lack of popular support.

And what's the matter with that? Shouldn't morality prevail over numbers? What about the civil rights movement? These brave souls, black and
white, who risked beatings by sitting in at southern lunch counters—weren't
they moral? The answer is, yes, they were. And weren't they outnumbered in
the South? Yes, they were.

So why shouldn't they have prevailed? The answer to this is that they *did*
prevail—over time. Lunch counters are no longer segregated by race. The

process of change was begun by a (locally) unpopular moral stand, but the success of that stand was achieved because a majority came to share it.

The process isn't automatic. The right to contend is not the right to prevail. People *should* take stands based on moral conviction, even if the stand is unpopular or illegal. It is the willingness to be reviled, to be imprisoned, that most dramatically makes the case to others. It is the strongest card that can be played, but it does not ensure that the hand soon will be won.

This is where the New Elite differs from the civil rights movement (or, for that matter, the Christian martyrs). The New Elite doesn't want to wait. Moral certainty should be enough. Faced with it, everyone else should fall in line—at once.

The problem of course is that the majority also has moral convictions. Sometimes, these conflict with the moral certainties of the educated elite. So who should prevail? Not always the majority. A necessary adjunct to majority rule is a written constitution guaranteeing certain inalienable rights. Even the expression of wildly unpopular views abhorrent to the majority is and should be protected by our Constitution.

But not all moral positions are protected by a written constitution. Most of them are fought out in the marketplace. The problem is, the New Elite has found a way around the necessity to compete. (Why compete with people less gifted? It takes a long time, and even worse, *they* might win.)

So this is how the new class handles moral disputes: each person's moral views should be respected. (So far, so good.) Each person's moral views should *prevail*. (Wait a second.)

Moral relativism says that we don't have to compete because each of us is right. Of course, those who say this don't really mean it. It's an excuse that permits them to pound the morality table for their own causes without having to listen to anyone else.

But that's not what they say. Instead, they say that morality is relative.

Moral relativists are not people who claim that there are two sides to every question. They're people who believe that there are no right answers to any question. They say "Your answer is as good as mine," by which they really mean that their own answer, however stupid or unprovable, is every bit as good as your answer, even if yours passes with flying colors the tests of logic, science, and history.

Moral relativists probably wouldn't insist that the world is flat, though in political and social and economic matters they often go further even than that. Everything that they say is always right, because to them there is no wrong. If you disagree with them, the closest they come to graciousness is to say that you're the victim of your culture. Which, somehow, they are not. Indeed, even though they're certain about everything, they're really, really certain about any view that offends the majority culture of their time and place.

Moral relativists believe that there are different truths for different people. What is true for you is not true for me. It's all relative.

It's all nonsense. What they are really saying is that there is no such thing as truth. No absolute truth. No absolute majority. Only different cultures. And if multiculturalism is desirable, well, then multimoralism must be desirable, too. Every culture must be respected (except, of course, one's own). So if a country views women as subhuman, denies them even the right to literacy, then we must respect that. Because everything is relative. What's wrong for us is right for them. There is no absolute right or wrong. All views, even contradictory ones, must be respected.

Just think about it. This view has pervaded the intellectual life of our time, and through it the popular culture. "If it works for you, it must be right." "What," you say, "even murder?" "Well, yes," is the reply, "under some circumstances, if society has embittered a person enough, then murder is understandable." Understandable. The moral relativists have just enough sense not to say it's good. But we know what they mean by "understandable." Perfectly.

By the dawn of the twenty-first century, moral relativism dominated public discourse. It was the underlying assumption of many of our leading "thinkers" and their leading thoughts. So dominant had this assumption grown within our culture that it was no longer enough to dissolve the difference between right and wrong. Now we have to blur as well the distinction between good and evil. Anything goes, just so long as the action was "understandable."

And then came 9/11. More than towers fell. It was no longer possible to see evil as merely an abstraction. It took that level of evil, children killed, children orphaned, not one murder but thousands, for all the fools finally to see that, yes, there is such a thing as pure evil. Absolute evil.

Soon after 9/11, an exhausted Mayor Rudy Giuliani addressed the General Assembly of the United Nations. It was a way of speaking to the world and saying what this all meant. And he did. He declared from the rostrum that "the era of moral relativism" must end. He went even further. He made a distinction between victim and murderer. Between good and evil. "We are right and they are wrong." He reminded the world that life is rational.

Of course, some things *are* relative. But good and evil are not among them. Sometimes, admittedly, it's difficult to see clearly what is good and what is its true opposite. And sometimes, as just now, it's impossible for decent people not to see it.

But doesn't believing in absolute morality make us no different than Osama bin Laden? No, it does not. Because we also believe in pluralism. We believe in absolutes when it comes to a moral code, but we don't believe in imposing our views on others, except through example and advocacy. Pluralism means that we respect others' beliefs, even when we think they're wrong. Moral relativism means that if we respect other people's morals and culture, it's because right and wrong do not exist. Of course, if you do believe in absolute right and wrong, but not in pluralism, then you're not actually a moral absolutist. You're merely a fanatic. A terrorist. Osama bin Laden is a fine example.

By labeling things objectively at last, the framework for moral obfuscation was gone. Objective reality has begun to return to public discourse.

★   ★   ★

The other effect of 9/11 was political. President Bush became a symbol of national unity. His popularity soared to the ionosphere and stayed there for a very long time.

The public response to his leadership has been somewhat misunderstood. Many commentators have said that Republicans have more credibility on defense issues, and Democrats on domestic issues, so Bush was dealt the perfect hand in personal and partisan terms.

There's some truth to this, but it's not the main point. The central reason for Bush's enormous popularity is that he is addressing a *national* issue, one that by definition affects all Americans. Until 9/11, we had been used to politicians (including Bush) who stitched together a quilt of very disparate patches to cover the body politic. A single issue here, a local subsidy there, and when the quilt grew large enough, one could claim that everyone had been taken care of.

Except they hadn't. While everyone received something, it wasn't the same thing. We all have special needs, but we have shared needs, too, and what was lacking from the American political scene was the sense of being addressed as voters *together*. Almost no one had been speaking of a *common* destiny. National security is an issue that embodies our American destiny. Had Gore been president on 9/11, that would still be true and he would have reaped much benefit.

The key to electoral popularity is to address everyone on the same subject at the same time. You can't win over 6 percent of the voters on one issue and

9 percent on another, until you get to 51 percent. That's not a true majority, which must at the very least share some belief in common. Either party can achieve such a majority. The economy is as inherently majoritorian an issue as national security. And there are others. Each is a key to the new political re-alignment aching to be formed.

In the politics of new class warfare, the worst thing that a politician can do is to betray the common interest for a specific tactical gain. In 2002, George Bush committed just such a gaffe when he supported high steel tariffs to keep one union happy. Everyone knows that Bush believes strongly in free trade. He was clearly departing from a majoritorian principle in order to line up the steelworkers' votes for the 2002 elections. In terms of public reaction, he got away with it, not because national security trumps all other issues, but because the Democrats let him get away with it. *They* wanted that union vote, too. Still, it was a mistake for both parties. (Bush later changed his position on steel tariffs, due to trade pressure.)

In the future, the party, the philosophy, and the candidates who will achieve and deserve ascendancy will be those who address the whole and not the parts. How tragic that it took a terrorist attack to show us what should always have been clear.

PART THREE

The Way We Vote Now

TEN

The New Way of Picking Presidents

We have seen that the growth of the New Elite—and the public's response to that growth—have completely transformed American politics. Issues no longer matter very much except as keys to the identity of the candidate. What every voter—New Elite or Left Behind—wants to know is how committed the candidate is to majority rule. Everyone seeking office still pays lip service to "the people," of course, so what they say in this regard has no meaning. (Indeed, one might note that the more frequently one invokes "the people," the less likely are the people in fact to be consulted—take, for example, the various people's republics so recently crumbled to dust.)

There is no issue save one: the identity of the candidate. Is the candidate part of the New Elite? Does the candidate go along with those who seek to avoid or evade the wishes of the majority? Does the candidate think that the majority is irrelevant—that decisions should be made by experts, not voters?

To answer these questions, the voters need to find out who the candidate really is. It's not a question of issues, but a quest for identity: who is the candidate? It does little good to know the candidate's stand on tariffs or taxes. What the voters desperately need instead is to discover the candidate's values. What people really want to know is whether the candidate has values—left or right, high or low, any values at all other than an unstated assumption that any problem can be solved if only the smartest people tackle it.

Every ad and every speech in every campaign are designed to show that the candidate is a man or woman of the people—sharing the values of most people and willing to be guided by those values. This is who candidates say they are. But once in office, they may turn out to be something else.

Just look at Jimmy Carter. He ran as a Georgia peanut farmer and ended up trying to solve all the problems of the ages through sheer application of intellect. After his administration ended in failure, one of his ablest aides, James

Fallows, wrote an article about what had happened. He called it "The Passionless Presidency." But that's not quite it. Carter's problem was not that he had no passion, but rather that he had no values. Actually, that's not quite it, either. He surely did have values but he didn't think it was fair to bring them to the table of decision. All that should be allowed to matter was ratiocination: if leaders are smart enough and think hard enough, they'll soon have all the answers.

In real life, of course, there have always been smart people on both sides of big issues. Of course, it's better to be smart than stupid; but in deciding whether welfare does more good than bad, we all vote our values. And so when somebody gets the calculator out—and nothing else—it does indeed seem like what's missing is passion. But in fact, alas, what's really missing is the voters.

Please note that the Carter presidency was followed by twelve years of Republican rule. To some, this was because Ronald Reagan was the "Great Communicator." To others, it was because the country had made an ideological turn to the right. But a look back at opinion and exit polls in the landmark election year of 1980 will show that what the Republicans really had going for them was that they weren't Democrats.

Certainly, Ronald Reagan wasn't Jimmy Carter. In fact, he seemed as different from Carter as any person possibly could. Carter thought that every problem could be solved by pure concentration of reason; Reagan relied on ideology. (He didn't call it ideology, or even philosophy, because these words carried a whiff of intellectual construct; he talked instead of his "beliefs.") Where Carter treated each issue as separate and distinct, to Reagan everything was related to a few basic principles. In her memoir of the Reagan years, speechwriter Peggy Noonan says that when she and her White House colleagues disagreed about what the true conservative response to a particular problem might be, they simply went and asked the president.

The fact that Reagan had a central philosophy—a fundamental set of values—explains much of his appeal. Politicians with an expressed philosophy are seeking the majority's support. They want to pull in all the fish with a single net rather than hook them one at a time. The New Elite does just the opposite: it legitimizes and promotes a reliance on single-issue politics. If one makes separate promises to enough single-issue groups, one can actually win an election—but not a true majority. Twelve percent of the fanatics on one issue and 5 percent on another and so on may add up to more than 50 percent on election day. But there is no majority that believes in the same thing. The 12 percent may have nothing in common with the 5 percent—each may well oppose the other's stand on its basic issue. One of the great appeals of single-issue politics to the New Elite is that it permits election to office without attracting a real majority. It bypasses—it denies—the formation of a true majority.

Reagan's wide net seemed to do just the opposite. He gave the appearance of proceeding from a few basic principles. Some of these principles were in fact contradictory—the belief that government should be limited is not easily compatible with laws prohibiting abortion. But Reagan's appeal stemmed from his promotion of broad principles, not specific positions. It was possible to see his abortion stance as stemming from his traditional values principle, rather than as capitulation to a single-interest group. It may seem strange to say that a public policy is much more acceptable, even to its opponents, if its basis is general principle rather than interest group pandering. But, as George H. W. Bush was later to discover, such is the case.

Reagan gave the impression of speaking to the whole country at once, of saying "This is what I believe and I hope that a majority of you agree with it." Carter often gave the impression of saying that five and twelve and ten and sixteen and eight add up to fifty-one. When Reagan rolled right over Carter in an electoral landslide, there were those who saw Americans as moving decidedly to the right, but this misses part of the point. A great many of those who voted for Reagan disagreed with some of his specific policies. There were in fact Reagan voters who were troubled by parts of his general philosophy. But almost all of them approved mightily of the fact that he seemed to *have* a general philosophy, that he was speaking to a whole rather than to a disparate collation of parts.

It was much more difficult then for a Democratic candidate to do this, even if one were so inclined. Reagan's election was made far easier by the exceptional visibility of single-interest factions within the Democratic Party. As noted, the 1972 "reforms" of the Democrats had guaranteed polarization. The efforts of the New Elite to transform each interest group into a political party of its own had been successful. Democratic National Conventions increasingly resembled the confrontation of warring tribes who had inadvertently rented the same hall. But the average voter hates single-issue politics, quite apart from distaste for fanaticism, because any party that permits it to flourish cannot possibly believe in majority rule. People prefer a majoritarian to an opponent who is not, even when they agree with the opponent on a number of important issues.

The public reaction that swept Reagan into office kept him there. He was reelected by the greatest electoral landslide of all time. Many ascribe the lop-sided result to the challenger's promise to raise taxes. This was undoubtedly a factor, but even more so was context. Walter Mondale had been vice president under Jimmy Carter, and Carter had seemed to many to be a New Elite president. Further, Mondale was a lifelong creature of the Democratic Party and therefore could not avoid seeming to embody what it had become. The constant need to negotiate positions with Jesse Jackson and labor leaders and gay leaders and feminists recharged the old suspicions of the Left Behinds, who had learned to see single-issue politics as an early-warning buzzer.

Four years later, the Republicans won another landslide victory, this time without Reagan. At the start of the campaign, Michael Dukakis actually led George H. W. Bush in the polls. By election day, however, Dukakis had been rejected in virtually every state. The reasons are instructive.

If one sentence can encapsulate sheer folly, it was Dukakis's bold assertion that "this campaign is about competence, not ideology." It was the perfect po-litical slogan of the New Elite. Whatever Dukakis meant to say, what he actu-ally seemed to be saying was this: I am smarter than my opponent and there-fore I should win, regardless of what either of us believes in. Issues don't matter. All that counts is pure IQ.

This is, of course, exactly what elections are now about. The voters want elections to be about ideology. About issues. About values. The voters are con-cerned about taxes and crime and health care and jobs and pollution. And they know that these issues are best addressed through the consistent applica-tion of values. They know that a fifteen-point spread in the Stanford–Binet score of the candidates is meaningless.

So George H. W. Bush became the president. The political scene had been transformed by the emergence of the New Elite and the general public's des-perate and confused reaction to it. But while this strange new political climate contributed to George Bush's victory, four years later it led to his defeat.

It is often noted that Bush's defeat stemmed in significant part from his re-treat from the pledge: "Read My Lips—No New Taxes." The fact that he agreed to some tax increases was not in itself fatal. Nor even was the spectacle of him breaking his word. What really hurt Bush was the seeming lack of a central philosophy. There may have been excellent short-term practical reasons for Bush to go along with the tax increase—but that's precisely what made him look bad. He seemed to be choosing competence over ideology, and his supporters thought the last election had decided that issue the other way.

When it came time to run for reelection, something else, too, helped to sink the president: he appeared to be the captive of the single-issue groups. In today's new climate, he couldn't have made a worse mistake.

Note that every election since 1972 has been decided by a frustrated and frightened electorate sensing retreat from majority rule. In each case, these disaffected votes are cast against the party that seems to be leading the retreat. And in three successive elections—1980, 1984, and 1988—their target was the Democrats (due in large part to the high visibility of single-issue groups within, if not over, the Democratic Party).

In 1992 that perception finally changed, in the Bush–Clinton race. Both candidates that year deserve some credit for this development. Just look at each during his own nominating convention. The Republican convention was a disaster. What everyone remembers are the speeches of the Religious Right. This was immensely damaging to Bush. What hurt was not so much the contents of the offending speeches—Reagan had used some of the same themes to boost his own popularity. Nor was it even a matter of tone—though the ugly edge to the speeches did not help. What really mattered was that the speakers gave the impression that the Republican Party had come under the control of single-issue groups.

The truth is that ever since the New Elite transformed American politics, both parties have been controlled to a significant degree by single-issue groups. These were all too visible within the Democratic Party. The Republicans had an equivalent problem with religious fundamentalists and the Pro-Life movement, but this wasn't nearly as apparent to the general public. The reason for the relative invisibility of these single-issue groups was Ronald Reagan. Because Reagan largely agreed with his party's single-issue groups, those factions weren't seen as pushing him to accept their agendas. They didn't have to confront him. He did promote their views, but when he did it seemed to be his own views that were being promoted.

With Bush it was quite different. When Pat Robertson and Pat Buchanan spoke at the Republican convention, few people thought that they spoke for Bush. Buchanan had just finished running a very negative campaign against the incumbent president in the primaries. It was widely reported that his prominence at the convention was part of his price for finally supporting Bush. The reason Buchanan's speech hurt Bush was not that people thought Bush agreed with it, but rather that they knew he did not. And so what was Buchanan doing up there in the spotlight? It seemed that the president didn't control his own party. It was controlled rather by single-issue groups, by fanatics. The specter of Bush having to negotiate his way through his own convention with factional leaders reminded people of all those Democratic candidates forced to put Jesse Jackson on in prime time.

Which brings us to Bill Clinton's nominating convention. For the first time in twelve years, Jesse Jackson was nowhere to be seen. And if his absence was too subtle a symbol, Clinton also made a point of blasting Sister Souljah for extreme remarks made during an appearance with Jackson.

The contrast between the two candidates could not have been greater. Bush seemed the captive of his party's extremists. Clinton drove the extremists out. Clinton's denunciation of Sister Souljah and his very public distancing of himself from Jackson were not matters of impulse. His actions in these matters were very carefully planned. They were part of a strategy that understood what really matters in elections held today, a strategy that produced the first Democratic presidential victory in sixteen years. This strategy was not disassociation from African Americans—Clinton was later to be called, by blacks, the first black president—but disassociation from extremists, from the strident leaders of single-issue groups.

It was a strategy that elected the second president of the United States who was arguably a member of the New Elite (Carter was, inarguably, the first). And it was accomplished by portraying him as just the opposite of who he was in fact.

★   ★   ★

William Jefferson Clinton, as all the world now knows, was born in relatively humble circumstances in Arkansas. His mother was a nurse and his father, a salesman, had died in a car accident before the baby was born.

That baby's astonishing success in the world was due primarily to his intellect. It was apparent at a very early age that Bill Clinton had remarkable political skills, boundless energy, and absolutely world-class charm. These attributes propelled his rise, but the motor of ascension was his intellect. When his public school teachers reported on young Bill's precocity, his mother, at some sacrifice, moved him to a private school. The boy with no real money or family connections went on through academic skill to achieve degrees from Georgetown, Oxford, and the Yale Law School. It was by any standard an exceptionally elite education. And it brought Bill Clinton into contact with an exceptionally elite group of classmates.

There was a time when if a poor but brilliant boy from Arkansas had been wafted up to Oxford and Yale, he would have fallen in with the scions of the American aristocracy, social and financial. But by the time Bill Clinton reached Yale, this had already greatly changed. His classmates now, a very great many of them, were members of a new elite. They were there not because grandfather had been there, or because father might donate a chapel. They were there for the same reason he was: they had done very well on tests.

What these new privileged students did was just what the old privileged students had done—they got to know one another. Many of them worked very hard at it. To use a word not yet then in vogue, they networked. This has always been one of the great opportunities of elite higher education: the chance for promising young people to form lifetime personal alliances through concentrated proximity with other members of their class.

Only now, it was a different class. Just as George H. W. Bush, the son of a Wall Street and social lion, during his years at Yale had become acquainted with hundreds of offspring similarly fortunate, so did Bill Clinton, one generation later at Yale Law School, get to network avidly with his own generational peers. But things had changed. A new class had emerged. Bush's peers were heirs; Clinton's were academic achievers. Far fewer of Clinton's classmates were the progeny of the rich. At Bush's Yale, the parents of the students often knew each other, too. Very few of the parents of Bill Clinton's new army of friends had ever met or heard of one another. Clinton's classmates were not from one social or financial class, or nearly so homogeneous in terms of geography, gender, religion, or race. Most of them were there almost exclusively because of extraordinary performance on the Law School Aptitude Test (a measure of innate ability, not education) and the thousand essays and final exams in the years that preceded it.

They were there because they were smart, and they were told this every day. Many bright students had been rejected so that the even brighter might be admitted. The handful who had made it were the result of a winnowing process that had begun in kindergarten. They were the few golden salmon who had survived the swim upstream. They were the best. And this was repeated to (and by) them with great frequency, as compliment and goad: they were the best. Everyone else had been left behind.

In past generations, students at the elite centers of higher education had also been instilled with a sense of being select. George H. W. Bush's classmates were told they were special, too. They fully expected to occupy the highest positions in society. At Groton and Andover, Princeton and Harvard, the carved names and fading portraits of statesmen and diplomats and captains of industry were everywhere, and when Tom or Dick spoke well in chapel or scored a touchdown, it was not rash to assume he'd be at least an undersecretary.

The New Elite shared the same high aspirations—expectations—but in a very different way. Preferment was no longer to be a matter of class privilege, but was based on individual merit. Advancement through connections was being replaced by advancement through proven merit.

This was, of course, absurd. What was in fact occurring was really just more of the same. The role of connections remained paramount. It still helped immensely to have been the new attorney general's former roommate. Some things never change.

But one thing had changed. The New Elite was able to fool itself. Its members were able to believe that their advancement was nothing more or less than merit finding its due reward. The role of connections, let alone the idea of connections based on class, did not have to be acknowledged, even to oneself. *Plus ça change, plus c'est la même chose*—only now those benefiting from the *même chose* didn't have to know it.

Today's cronyism is much easier—and more flagrant—because those who assist their friends no longer have to think of it as cronyism. In the old days, it was a little embarrassing to tap Tom or Dick just because one had been with them at Yale. But the New Elite can continue the practice while abandoning the guilt. One isn't picking Tom or Dick just because they were at Yale. One is picking only the brightest. And that's (supposedly) been certified by the fact that Tom or Dick was admitted to Yale. This way of looking at it makes all the difference. One can appoint as many of one's classmates as one wishes and think of it as a dispassionate quest for merit.

If Bill Clinton was at the center of a vast New Elite network, then how could he be elected president? The simple answer is that that's not the way he was portrayed by his campaign. Clinton ran as a man of the people, as a majoritarian and a centrist. The campaign was very effective. Its strategy was devised and carried out by James Carville, a shrewd New Orleans politician whose nickname was "the ragin' Cajun." If there were a Mount Rushmore for Left Behinds, Carville's head would be there. (The cigar might take some doing.) He was pure politician. Pure and simple—he kept the campaign on first principles. It was Carville who wrote on the headquarters' wall the great imperative of the campaign: "It's the economy, stupid." What he meant, of course, was that the key to victory was talking about the economy. There were to be no more pronouncements on trendy social issues, no costly courting of factional leaders, and certainly no preference for competence over ideology.

The idea was to talk to the whole country at the same time. And the issue that had everyone's full attention was the economy. In addition, if you were always talking about the economy, then you couldn't be talking about all the other issues that were high priorities for the single-issue groups but proven poison to the voters. It was a complete reversal for the Democratic strategy of the previous three presidential campaigns.

And when Carville said, "It's the economy, stupid," just whom do you suppose he meant by "stupid"? Why, all those really smart folks from Yale, not to mention all those Rhodes scholars hanging around the headquarters and drinking cappuccino. It was the exasperation of a natural pol for the blunders of overeducated fools. And the country knew exactly what he was talking about.

Carville's advice worked. Far more amazing, his advice was taken. The Clinton campaign had been so rocked by scandal and mishap that the policy wonks turned desperately to someone whose pulse was that of the people.

There was a time in American history when the candidate himself was the real politician, intuitively in touch with the popular will. Candidates knew how to get elected, but often were less alert about what to do thereafter. So they surrounded themselves with experts, policy mavens to whom programs were catnip and small print deep clover. These experts wrote the position papers and came up with the detailed programs and answered the questionnaires from the editorial boards.

That was then. But things change. By the time of Clinton's campaign, it was the candidate who was the policy expert, an addict whose true fast-food craving was for details. And it was Carville's, and later Dick Morris's, job to know what the voters wanted. With today's political parties little more than holding pens for single-issue groups, it is possible even for longtime office-holders not to have a clue as to the yearnings of the electorate. So modern candidates hire "experts," not on issues but on people. In this reversal alone, one can sense the astonishing upheaval in American politics that has flowed from the emergence of the New Elite.

Another aspect of the vastly altered political climate is that the voters have become less able to vote on the basis of issues. They're too busy looking for clues as to the candidate's true identity—is this an expert who thinks he's been certified to give us all the answers, or is this really one of us except for the Armani suit? Much of what voters now must do is search for clues to help answer this question. They want to know whether the candidate is part of the New Elite or the Left Behinds. So lifestyle clues are very important—is there some adherence to tradition or has everything in life just been invented anew? Is the candidate's primary identity with his roots or with his peers?

This is what the voters are really looking for today. And it helps explain why the only two successful Democratic candidates in nearly thirty years were governors who came from small southern towns. The fact that they were governors meant that they weren't from Washington, D.C., a city of fifty thousand lawyers and no voters. It also meant that they were still living in the states where they were born. They lived their lives surrounded by real people, or so it was supposed. As for their upbringing, it is scarcely possible to imagine environments further removed from the enclaves of meritocracy than Plains, Georgia, and Hope, Arkansas. Small towns win extra points in the voters' search for clues. It's not unreasonable to see them as incubators of majoritarian sentiments—not because small towns are classless (they are highly stratified)—but because everyone knows everyone else and it's impossible to avoid a sense of the whole.

Both Jimmy Carter and Bill Clinton had roots that were vastly reassuring. This was a major factor in their winning enough primaries to emerge as their party's nominee. Early on, however, the Clinton pollsters were amazed to discover that the public had their candidate all wrong. It seems that a surprisingly large number of voters thought that Clinton was a child of privilege, born into a family of wealth and influence. This perception stemmed from a heavy emphasis on the candidate's superb education. It stemmed from the flaunting of his vast network of influential friends. It was the way he looked and talked. All of these indicia once upon a time would have been signs of patrician birth; in today's world, though, they merely bespoke a high IQ. Clinton was something of a harbinger, and much of the public mistakenly placed him as a scion of the old elite.

Carville fixed that. The shaded streets of Hope were soon crowded with documentary camera crews. Huck Finn would seem to be of royal birth compared with the plucky barefoot lad in all the testimonials run on every network. These commercials were not deceptive. Clinton did indeed ascend from humble rural roots. His rise was due not only to natural ability but to very hard work. Let there be no mistake: his hard-won success is commendable. The point is merely that the fruits of that success, so easily mistaken for the trappings of hereditary privilege, were the contemporary rewards of a large and growing meritocracy. Bill Clinton was not Horatio Alger, whose drive took him from poverty to full membership in an old elite. The members of Clinton's glittering circle were for the most part as new to privilege as he.

They had been Rhodes scholars, too. It's no longer just a handful who rise up to join the establishment: it's a whole new establishment.

Understandably, the Clinton campaign talked about roots and not branches. It was "the Man from Hope," not Merton College, who was featured in the ads. The consistent and incessant portrayal was of an Arkansas boy who was true to his origins and close to his neighbors. The public saw a candidate whose career had been spent entirely in Arkansas. He had been re-elected governor several times by the people of that small and poor and populist state. The American voting public, increasingly sensitive to danger signs of New Elite allegiance, was reassured by the image of Clinton that they were shown.

They weren't quite so sure about the candidate's wife. In the search for identity, the biggest blip on the public's radar screen was Hillary Clinton's comment about making cookies. She had been questioned incessantly about possible conflicts of interest that might arise if she practiced law in any large firm in the state her husband governed. Understandably exasperated and surely exhausted, she snapped back, "What do you expect me to do—stay home and bake cookies?"

This rejoinder received more attention than the call for term limits. Everyone was talking about it. The problem was not that Ms. Clinton was a working mother. Millions—tens of millions—of American mothers held down jobs. The problem was not that the first lady of Arkansas had chosen to be a full-time attorney. The fact that a woman of her age and education had chosen not to be a full-time homemaker was scarcely exceptional. But what really mattered was the suspicion that she disapproved of that traditional role. It was possible to read her words as scornful, derisive to those who had failed to choose a career.

This was probably a bum rap. The context of her remarks was the implication that anything she did would conflict with her husband's high office. Presumably, that included civic activities and any expression of opinion. No wonder she was exasperated. It is also an incontrovertible fact that Ms. Clinton (or Rodham, as she may have been at the time), like most working mothers, devoted extraordinary time and energy to the care and maintenance of her family. In addition to providing most of her family's income, she was by every account its vital center.

But the fact remains that she caused an explosion. The public had become highly sensitized to signs of elitist disdain. Many people sensed the emergence of a new professional class that felt itself superior to those of lesser educational attainment. In this new climate of anxiety and resentment, the supposed deprecation of traditional homemaking as opposed to the practice of corporate law was exactly the sort of land mine whose shrapnel would cause maximum damage. The fact that the wife of the candidate may have held no such elitist views was irrelevant. There were so many open wounds that little salt was needed.

Despite events of this sort, however, candidate Clinton frightened fewer voters than had any of the three Democrats who ran for president before him. He ran very specifically as a "new Democrat," which everyone took to mean moderate, majoritarian, traditional, and free from faction. He seemed more apart from allegiance to the new class than did his ill-fated predecessors. He kept stressing one theme, the economy, and by doing so avoided pushing all the peripheral buttons that detonate Left Behind rage.

And he was lucky in his opposition. President George Herbert Walker Bush failed to articulate a single majoritarian theme and emerged from a convention that seemed to be controlled by single-issue factions of the right. Put all these things together, and it added up to the first presidential election in many years in which the Democratic candidate didn't seem closer to the antimajoritarians than his opponent.

Even so, Clinton barely won. The electorate remained suspicious. One last factor made Clinton's election possible: the candidacy of Ross Perot. Perot emerged as the candidate of the middle-class Left Behinds. He ran as an antielitist, and his greatest appeal was to those who sensed that decision making somehow was being taken out of the hands of the people. Whatever Perot did or did not have in mind, his followers were often fueled by resentment of a new emergent class. There was a great deal of the Who-Are-These-Smart-Guys-Who-Are-Trying-to-Tell-the-Rest-of-Us-What-to-Do? in Perot's approach and his appeal.

Populist candidates have emerged in the past to challenge the hegemony of elites, and the essence of populist revolt is the little guys against the big forces. It is instructive that now the challenger was a billionaire. No one seemed to think it strange that one of the richest men in the world was one of the little guys. Yet this was something very new. The reason no one questioned it was that there was nothing to question: in today's altered hierarchy, it is possible to have several billion dollars and still be, or feel oneself to be, outside the dominant elite.

The destruction of our political parties by the New Elite created a large new pool of homeless voters from which Perot drained much support. He attracted refugees from both parties, but exit polls showed that more defected from Bush than from Clinton. If Perot had not run, Bush would have won. As it was, Clinton was elected with just 43 percent of the vote. This isn't as fractious as France in 1954, but neither is it the voice of a true majority. And it does suggest why independent Jesse Ventura years later was elected governor of Minnesota.

Whatever the percentage, Clinton did win. The candidate became the president. And so he said goodbye to his campaign manager. James Carville went off to tell still other candidates what real voters were like. The new president was not left alone, however. He had many, many friends. Indeed, he was perhaps the most ardent networker of his generation. As a callow youth en route to Oxford, he had not wasted his solitary evening in New York before the boat sailed; he somehow managed to have dinner with the editor of *Harper's*. His pace never slackened, and by the time of the presidential campaign, everyone knew that FOB meant "friend of Bill." It seemed at times that everyone was an FOB—everyone, that is, who'd emerged from the ivyest groves of academia clutching the most glittering prizes. It was perhaps the most astonishing collection of frenetic overachievers ever to be bound together by acquaintance with the same disarming friend.

And now they all were FOPs—friends of the president. And in a sense, they were the presidency, this vast constellation of the most glittering stars. They were the pool of talent, the newest generation's Best and Brightest, this time around with fewer corporate stars and more law professors but at least as assured as their predecessors of their proven capacity to govern. They were not only the talent pool, they were both sounding board and filter for the program and the personnel by which this presidency would leave its mark.

Six months after his election, President Clinton had the lowest approval rating of any new president since the advent of national polling. Gaffe followed gaffe on an almost daily basis. Appointments were withdrawn amid anger and derision. Every land mine scattered throughout the political landscape seemed to have been stomped upon. Pundits and public alike were howling over blunders and ineptitude.

How had such disaster befallen a president with so many glittering advisers? Because all that glitters is not gold. Those around Clinton, all the gifted FOBs, were indeed smarter than hell, but in touch, as it turns out, primarily with one another. This is central to Clinton's early unpopularity. Governing well, governing at all, means being in touch with the electorate. It doesn't mean doing whatever the opinion polls show to be popular at a given moment, but decidedly it does mean knowing what people want. And feel. And value.

Knowing what people are thinking has nothing to do with IQ. But it's not entirely instinctive, either. It's related to experience. It's not merely a question of knowing lots of people, but of knowing people different from oneself. Until quite recently, we could gather a sense of what other people were like simply by being with them in a neighborhood or workplace. But no more. Now people live and work with others very much like themselves in terms of perceived intelligence, and therefore education, and therefore income. Everyone they know has had experiences much like their own.

The late populist philosopher Eric Hofer liked to tell the story of a professor of mathematics at Berkeley. Before China and the United States were on speaking terms, this American professor was selected by the Chinese to describe his countrymen to their own vast population. The professor gladly complied. He wrote that Americans were mean-spirited, untrustworthy, treacherous, devious, cruel, and capable of stabbing even lifelong friends in the back. This description was widely circulated throughout China. How, Hofer asked, was it possible to characterize Americans in this way, when in fact they were the least suspicious and most generous people on earth? He couldn't understand it. And then it came to him: "The professor was talking about the mathematics department at Berkeley!"

We are all the victims of our own experience. If we live and work with people very much like ourselves, this cannot help but color our view of human nature. So if something is acceptable to us (the extended me), then it's presumed to be acceptable to everyone else as well. There is no capacity at all for anticipating a contrary perception.

The problems arising from this insularity began to be apparent as soon as the election was over. It was not necessary to wait even for the inaugural. The Clinton team—Carville gone, the FOBs clogging all roads to Washington—announced a summit conference on the economy. Hundreds of experts were summoned to testify. Presentations of dazzling complexity were revealed at marathon sessions lasting late into the night. Sitting in the midst of all activity, questioning and listening, recording and correcting, acting as moderator, facilitator, and depository, was none other than the president-elect. Press and participants alike were dazzled by his tireless mastery of detail, his own vast expertise that often seemed to surpass that of the distinguished presenters. It was the nation's most distinguished seminar, and its star was unarguably the smiling yet thoughtful Arkansan.

Yet despite the kudos for Clinton's performance, the public seemed unmoved. In fact, there was a sense of unease. Many of those close to Clinton were astonished that their own enthusiasm seemed so narrowly shared. It didn't make sense to them. The president-elect had been terrific. Weren't people watching?

Many people had been watching. And while the opinion was universal that the president was very smart, quite a few observers wondered why this conference had been called. Clinton had won in part because he had kept talking about one issue that touched all lives: the economy. So it was reasonable to presume that he had a view on this issue. Put another way, this was the big issue to which the candidate, if elected, would bring his values. Well, he was elected. But where were those values? What were they? Why was he consulting all those experts? Didn't he know himself where he wanted to go? The slogan had not been "It's the Economic Summit, stupid." Everything he wanted to do seemed to proceed from data, not principle.

The sense of unease began to focus, and not for the better. The very first steps of the new administration seemed to take it further and further from the locus of majoritarian concern.

Once Clinton had taken the oath of office, the first big issue he advanced was equal treatment for gays in the military. This provoked an angry public reaction. It is important not to misunderstand the nature of this anger. While undoubtedly some of it was due to antigay prejudice, there were more powerful components. At the heart of the protest was the feeling that this was a peripheral issue. It did not seem to directly affect the lives of most Americans. And since it was the first initiative of the new administration, one could assume that it had the highest priority. This was the real problem. The emphasis seemed to be on placating a single-issue group, rather than on addressing the concerns of the average citizen.

Of course, the timing of the Clinton proposal probably was unrelated to its importance within the administration. Perhaps there was a desire to get the issue out of the way as soon as possible. Whatever the motive, or lack thereof, it seems unlikely that the administration had any idea of the firestorm that its proposal would ignite.

Much of the opposition had nothing to do with the issue of gay rights. It was directly related to the fear and suspicion that Left Behinds hold for the New Elite. It was the fear not of sexual orientation, but of government without consent. It was anger against the candidate who was elected to address the problems of the average voter but was now addressing something else. People weren't so mad at what Clinton was proposing as at what he appeared not to be.

That the Clinton proposal did not enjoy the support of the majority of Americans is not relevant to this discussion. There is no reason for a majoritarian to advocate only what is already popular. A president should lead, even when the cause is unpopular. In this regard, Clinton was correct to compare his proposal to Harry Truman's racial integration of the armed services. Both presidents did what they thought was right and knew to be controversial.

But the comparison is not perfect. Truman acted by executive order. His decision was a fait accompli. Clinton chose to court congressional approval. This guaranteed that public attention was focused on the issue; and that, plus its timing at the very beginning of the administration, made it seem the highest priority of the incoming president.

Also, as the saying goes, Bill Clinton was no Harry Truman. Even in the days when Truman was unpopular, no one ever thought of calling him an elitist. It was hard to see him as out of touch with the average citizen. Clinton, however, was for most Americans at best a clean slate and, at less than best, the embodiment of government by experts. The composition of the armed services did not affect people like Clinton and his friends, but it clearly did affect the lives of those whose backgrounds were similar to Truman's.

And one more thing: the changing status of interest groups within the Democratic Party. Both Truman and Clinton were professional politicians. Black voters had been absolutely essential to Truman's upset election victory in 1948, and gay voters were exceptionally helpful to Clinton in 1992. Each president could easily be seen as paying off a campaign debt. However, Truman was perceived as acting on principle, as saying to the majority, "This is what I intend to do; if you don't like it, vote for someone else." His action, though unpopular, was within the majoritarian system. Clinton, however, had publicly promised a gay audience before his election that he would lift the ban on gays in the armed forces. In today's world of single-issue dominance, Clinton looked like all those (defeated) Democratic candidates who danced only to strings pulled by interest groups. While in Truman's day the Democratic Party had at least a sense of confederation, by Clinton's time a balkanization had occurred, with each disparate part of the old empire claiming its own sovereignty. Even when acting in much the same way, Truman was seen as partisan and Clinton as factional.

The difference, of course, is perception. On the merits, Clinton's advocacy of gays in the military may have been more consistent with majority rule than

Truman's integration order. After all, Clinton had made his commitment publicly and before the election. Citizens strongly opposed were free to vote against him solely on this issue (and presumably some did). Further, Clinton did not operate through direct order; he consulted with an elected body—the Congress. He was clearly seeking the consent of the governed. But perception is all. Truman's action, popular or not, was seen as mainstream, and Clinton's was seen as symbolic of the postpolitical world of those who scorn majority rule. The suspicion began to grow that Clinton was not the New Democrat as promised, but subject to the same antimajoritarian forces that had ensnared Carter, Mondale, and Dukakis.

What truly fanned these flames of doubt was not an issue but an appointment. Clinton put forward the name of Zoe Baird for the post of U.S. attorney general. Her academic résumé was at least as impressive as that of the new president. She had testimonials from the most distinguished leaders in the land. Yet her name was soon met with howls of protest, and confirmation became so hopeless that no vote was ever taken: her name was withdrawn. The earthquake of indignation proceeded from a single fault: the nominee had failed to withhold taxes for her nanny.

People in other countries couldn't believe that such a star could fall for such a reason. Some people in this country couldn't believe it, either, but in many cases they, too, had nannies whose taxes were unpaid. It is impossible to understand what all the fuss was about without acknowledging the growing class fissure in America. Society has always known tension between the haves and the have-nots. Class resentment has always been with us. And as times change, the focus of resentment keeps pace. New symbols fit new classes. For many exhausted wage earners, the top hat has been replaced by the nanny as the symbol of what's gone wrong.

But if the nanny is a symbol of privilege, far more so is the failure to pay taxes for that privilege. It isn't a question of the rich being above the law—Leona Helmsley had already proved that there is accountability. But it is fair to say that the rules of our very complex society do not fall equally on all citizens. Those with high professional skills, and the capacity to hire other skilled professionals, can become more relaxed about following the rules. If they miss a deadline, they know about extensions. If they write an overdraft, the bank will cover it. If the deduction is disallowed, so be it. However, this margin of comfort is not felt by most of the populace. If a secretary writes an overdraft, she may lose her access to credit. Deadlines and limits and rules are immutable to most people, which is why there was so much outrage over the check-bouncing revelations of the House of Representatives.

The relevance of the Zoe Baird nomination is not that it engendered so much protest. Its significance is not the outburst, but the fact that no one saw it coming. The many advisers and FOBs in and near the White House didn't have a clue. The issue was raised and discussed and determined not to be that serious. On the merits, of course, this may well have been right. The infraction was inadvertent, minor, and eventually rectified. What remains astonishing is that there was no one available in the new governing class who had any idea of what the public's reaction would be. There was no one in touch with the people. As soon as members of the Senate were told about the tax problem, they predicted disaster. These were people who run for election. But there are only 537 of those in Washington (counting the president and vice president). Everybody else is either hired or appointed. And of this vast throng, the higher echelons are crowded with members of the New Elite.

Clinton spoke, no doubt genuinely, of his desire to bring more diversity to government. It is admirable to bring into power more women and people of color. And he did so. He called his cabinet the most diverse in American history. But the case can be made that it was also the least diverse. So many of the key players in the administration were alike in education and income and experience removed from the marketplace. Their failure to predict the Zoe Baird catastrophe was a sure sign of the absence of diversity—of everyone belonging to the same class, sharing the same perceptions and values, and being shaped more by that class than by the other characteristics that supposedly differentiated them.

The Zoe Baird nomination was followed by Kimba Wood's nomination for the same post. Once again, public outcry drove the nominee out of the field—this time, supposedly, for having hired an illegal alien. Wood, who arguably never violated any law, claimed she had disclosed every detail of her employer records to the administration. The continued virulence of the public reaction was a sign that some terrible built-up emotions had found at last an outlet for release. And the failure of the Clinton team to anticipate this outburst a second time, however slight the provocation, underscores yet again how out of touch the New Elite is with the Left Behinds. Disraeli spoke of the Two Englands, one rich and one poor, whose inhabitants were so dissimilar that they could be said to live in different nations. The same seems true of this new class division, based not on wealth but on measurable ability.

But the appointment that tells the story best was not for attorney general. It was for a slightly lesser but still very important post, the assistant attorney general for civil rights. The president nominated his classmate from the Yale Law School, University of Pennsylvania law professor Lani Guinier (now a member of the Harvard Law School faculty).

Professor Guinier was exceptionally well educated and taught at an Ivy League law school. She was the author of many scholarly works. Her experience in the field of civil rights law was virtually peerless. Yet her nomination also imploded. The outcry was so great that the president asked his old friend to withdraw her name, and when she refused to do so, he withdrew it himself.

The problem this time was not nannies. It was ideas. Professor Guinier had many original ideas in the area of voting rights. She questioned the efficacy of majority rule. She posited the possibility of alternative systems, such as weighted voting. She did not hide her views, but published them in scholarly journals.

In themselves, Professor Guinier's views were neither shocking nor subversive. Other estimable scholars have tinkered with the architecture of majority rule. But Professor Guinier had been nominated to head not a seminar, but the Civil Rights Division of the Department of Justice. She would be the nation's principal legal officer in charge of interpreting and advocating the voting rights of all citizens. To appoint to such a position one who sought alternatives to majority rule was shocking. And many were shocked.

Though, again, not the Clinton team. All the White House lawyers and scholars who had considered the nomination had let it go forward. Presumably, the retreat from majoritarian principles did not ring any alarm bells within the new class of advisers to the administration. It was only when Vice President Gore (previously a senator and so cognizant of the voters of Tennessee) read a magazine article about Professor Guinier's views and rushed in to see the president that the nomination was arrested. President Clinton actually took the time to read the offending articles by Guinier and then decided he must withdraw her name. Like the vice president, he had run for office in a southern state.

Think about this. The two highest officials in the land had to sit themselves down and peruse law journals because no one else on their staff seemed capable of seeing how explosive that fine print would be. It's hard to imagine a more dramatic example of the insularity—and power—of the New Elite than this spectacle of a huge, superbly educated vetting organization unable to discern any problem with a voting rights enforcer who would forestall majority rule. If its closest thing to Paul Revere was Al Gore, then this administration was in serious trouble.

President Clinton, of course, did see the problem when the articles were brought to his attention. So is it really fair to characterize him as a member of the New Elite? A better question is whether the president can be distinguished from the presidency. Can any individual be defined outside the context of his or her acquaintanceships, if that circle is homogeneous and self-chosen? Each of us is defined by our experience and dependent on others for information. True, a strong individual can of course choose his or her own coterie, and this Clinton had done. And not everyone within his circle was a member of the New Elite. As White House chief of staff he named Mac McCarty, a boyhood friend from Hope, Arkansas. Fortunately, Clinton, a tireless extrovert, knew people from every walk of life. Yet to the outsider, it seemed the preponderance of FOBs were people who, like Clinton himself, were pursuing professional careers launched by exceptional academic achievement. Their talents had been certified not in the marketplace but on the campus.

We have seen that whether one is a member of the New Elite or the Left Behinds is largely a matter of self-definition. But, very frequently, people are not honest with themselves about who they really think they are. Almost no one would answer "yes" if asked, "Are you a member of the new class that defines itself primarily by measurable intelligence?" Most of the members of the New Elite probably would say "no." And they would not be lying—at least not to others. But self-definition doesn't work that way. People don't define themselves as selfish or arrogant, though many are. Similarly, there is such a heavy bias in our culture against elitism that few would confess, even to themselves, such an allegiance.

Being a member of the New Elite is not like belonging to a secret society of conspirators. There's nothing sinister about it. There's nothing evil about being proud of one's ability and that of one's friends. There's nothing unusual about liking people who resemble oneself. It's perfectly natural to develop values based on one's own experience. It's surely forgivable to be ignorant of the values and perceptions of those we have never known. But the result of these normal reactions is the development of a uniform outlook. There now are millions of citizens, decent and thoughtful, who at an operative level feel with deep conviction that the big decisions must be decided by themselves and not the majority.

But back to Bill Clinton. Few who chose—with gusto and pride—the career of politician can unequivocally be described as a member of the New Elite. But by choosing to associate primarily with those of the same quantifiable skills, Clinton committed himself to a shared outlook. And he certainly seemed to believe that any problem could be solved if only the smartest people really studied it. One need merely collate all the data, however extensive, and then have the best minds absorb and analyze the data as never before, and then the problems of the ages will be solved by legislation.

Health care is a good example. Clinton the campaigner won ovations when he declared, "Health care in America is a disgrace." Everyone applauded, but not for the same reasons. There were those who thought he meant that health care was too expensive. Others were certain that what Clinton meant was that everyone should be covered by a health care program. Perhaps the candidate meant both things at the same time. As president, he proposed a health care package that he claimed would both extend coverage and lower costs. It was quite a challenge, but Clinton felt up to it.

Hundreds of experts pored over the data for months. Generally, when government tackles a major domestic problem it does so by choosing one value over another. For example, a Democrat might choose universal coverage as the highest value, a Republican lower cost. But the idea of choosing all values simultaneously is something new, suggesting that choice, that values, are not necessary: expertise alone can make everything better. If this proves to be the case, we will all benefit. If it does not—as it has not since time began—we can only conclude that the solution of a public problem requires placing some priorities higher than others. This is why voters must be concerned with ideology and not merely competence.

The belief in government by expertise has as a corollary an incapacity to treat the nation's problems as a whole. This is itself ancillary to the new class unwillingness to see the nation as a whole, rather than as a collection of interests and ethnic entities. And it is why Thomas L. Friedman, a superb commentator for the *New York Times*, could write in his analysis of the president's first year in office: "Mr. Clinton is like a doctor who prescribes one drug for backaches, another for knee joints, another for headaches. Each prescription alone promises relief from a particular symptom. Yet without a full diagnosis of where the nation is and why it needs to take such medicines, his prescriptions can also seem confusing and lack authority, and it is not at all clear the public will swallow them."

This was written after Clinton had just finished his most successful month in office, a month in which he had achieved several hard-won and admirable victories against fanatic single-issue opposition. This reversal of his fortunes in midcourse should not be seen as accidental.

We have seen that the early days of the Clinton administration were marked with numerous and consequential gaffes and symbols that outraged the general public. The contention is that this unrelenting stream of error can be traced to an administration constituted for the most part by members of a single new class and consequently incapable of judging the needs or reactions of those outside that class.

For those skeptical of this thesis, please note the appearance on the scene of a new presidential adviser. After months of sinking polls and scathing late show monologues, the desperate new president announced a major change in his staff. There was going to be a new chief adviser. His name produced gasps from the press.

It was not that David Gergin was inexperienced. Quite the contrary. He had performed a similar senior advisory function for Ronald Reagan. He was a lifelong Republican. On a major public television program devoted to examining current issues, he was the conservative whose job was to take on the liberal. There was so much attention paid to who he was that it was easy to overlook who he was not. He was not, in temperament or outlook, like the hundreds of FOBs in Washington. He was not disdainful of the marketplace, including the marketplace of public opinion. He was not, as the saying goes, a policy wonk. He was not an expert—except in the sense that James Carville had been an expert: he knew how to find the pulse of public opinion. He was in touch with the average voter.

With Carville's knowledge of what the people wanted, candidate Clinton had gone from a losing campaign to victory. Carville had instinctively known the public's hostility to interest group displacement of majority rule. The most deliberate, premeditated, and successful tactic of the Clinton campaign had been the public distancing of the candidate from Jesse Jackson.

After Gergin came aboard, Clinton became once again the majoritarian willing to stand up to special-interest groups. The most dramatic example of this was his strong leadership in the passage of NAFTA. It was not only that the NAFTA treaty would benefit the country as a whole rather than one region or constituency. What really helped Clinton was the opposition to his stand by leaders of various interest groups. He remained resolute on NAFTA, proclaiming its long-term public good, despite highly publicized attacks by the AFL–CIO, Ralph Nader, Pat Buchanan, and the Sierra Club! It is scarcely possible to imagine more dramatic or effective symbolism. And, though a clear majority of Americans did not support NAFTA, the president's popularity rose appreciably after its passage. People applauded Clinton, as they had Reagan, for seeming to work for the common good—whether or not they agreed with a specific measure.

ELEVEN

The New Elite in the White House

Defenders of Bill Clinton scoff at the idea that he personifies membership in a new elite class. This man, they say, is no haughty nerd; this is Bubba. This is the kid who tooled around Hot Springs with hot springs, lining the bed of his pickup truck with Astroturf. This is no wine-and-brie taster; this is the jogger who never made it past a golden arch. This is surely no scholar disdainful of the mob: Did you ever see this guy work a crowd?

But to say these things is to say nothing. To be a member of a class and to share its basic outlook and values doesn't mean losing all individual characteristics. It's not like *Invasion of the Body Snatchers;* no one gets taken over by a pod. You can still be fun. But what you can't be is all that different from your peers—at least the people you think are your peers. It doesn't matter where you come from; it's a question of where you think you belong now. You are what you meet. And if everyone you meet and know and enjoy and live with shares the same outlook, then after a while you do, too.

This is no conspiracy. It's simply the way life works. People with the same identity and economic interest and experience tend to see things the same way. Shared experience and shared identity lead to shared values. This is true of Irish cops in Queens and of Yale law graduates in Washington. They tend to see politics the same way, too.

Which brings us back to Bill Clinton. Everything—good and bad—about his presidency reflected his class perceptions. If you want to know what this new class thinks and wants and does and believes, look not necessarily at Clinton himself, but at the Clinton presidency.

In a number of ways, that presidency shows us what the new class stands for:

AVOIDANCE OF RISK

This is one of the hallmarks of the New Elite, one of its most fundamental values. It could scarcely be any other way. The New Elite's rewards come from testable talents, and generally this means professional careers. These rewards vary greatly by profession, of course, but seldom approach the brass rings for which real entrepreneurs are grasping. Comfort, not luxury, is the usual prize, further enhanced by a reduction of risk. To a stratified meritocracy, such a trade-off is attractive, since to them risk holds less opportunity than it does danger. The New Elite seeks to do well the precise jobs for which they were trained. Change is the enemy, and risk is its agent.

The Clinton presidency was severely damaged by its inherent abhorrence of risk. This is true at every level, in matters large and small. An obvious example is its slowness in making major appointments. Many top positions in the Justice Department, and in the federal judiciary itself, remained unfilled for unconscionable periods. When a vacancy occurred on the Supreme Court, the process of selecting a replacement seemed endlessly protracted. Months went by as trial balloons were launched, lists leaked, and decisions delayed. For to make a choice is to risk making a mistake. Granted, any administration whose opening salvo was Zoe Baird was entitled to be a little gun-shy. But it wasn't only the big, publicized posts that remained unfilled. The whole administration seemed paralyzed by the prospect of appointment. The fear of risk was obvious.

At this point, some partisan is surely pointing to the president's early health care proposal. Wasn't that taking a risk? Well, no, it really wasn't. There is no inherent risk in tackling subjects others have avoided—be it health care or welfare reform or crime. Risk consists not in placing such problems on the agenda, but in making hard choices to forward their solution. There is no real risk in saying that health care costs must be cut and coverage extended. This is win–win: the stingy and the needy are equally grateful. Of course, there is a risk in making promises if it turns out they can't be kept. But with vast new programs, the results aren't clearly known until the president is out of office and busy planning his library. In the short run, there is only credit for good intentions.

Real risk involves not simply stating what the problem is, and that the best minds in the land will resolve it, but also announcing which priority should prevail in its solution. When you put one priority first, then all the other priorities have to line up behind it, and what ends up last on your list may be first on somebody else's. And that makes some people mad. So a true risk avoider is for all priorities simultaneously. This approach benefits enormously from smoke and mirrors, and a prepaid ticket out of town.

Domestic issues can be addressed (for a while, anyway) without risk merely by being for everything good at the same time. Foreign policy, however, is quite another matter. Action is often required right away. To send in troops or not to send them, to applaud a coup or to oppose it, to impose sanctions or to increase aid, to ally here and oppose there: these are choices unprotected by the luxury of indolence. The choices must be made at once, and the cost of each risk is often human life.

This is one reason (others will be shown as well) why the Clinton administration neglected to such an astonishing degree any real engagement in foreign affairs. The risks of decision simply were too great. Of course, the risks of doing nothing are also vast, but to the mind-set of the New Elite, safely cocooned since the first SAT test, any motion for extension is preferable to having the jury come back into the box.

There is no virtue to bellicosity in global affairs. Long-range strategy is of course preferable to the quick fix. But there is a difference between caution and neglect. The New Elite and its exemplars fear not the wrong choice but choice itself. In foreign affairs, its dominant impulse is avoidance. The score is posted too quickly, and so they choose to stay home from the game.

GOVERNMENT BY EXPERTS

We have alluded to the tireless economic summit that preceded the Clinton inaugural. Despite, or perhaps because of, its findings, this cloistered symposium became the harbinger of—indeed, the metaphor for—the way this administration approached the task of governing.

The basic assumption seems to be that the experts know best. The problems of the ages remained unsolved because the best people weren't in charge. Experts have impeccable academic credentials and no ties to the electorate, which ensures "objectivity." If enough experts get together, long enough and preferably in a closed room, and really dig into the data . . . well, the rest is easy.

No one could invent an example of this procedure more glaringly illustrative than the health care task force. Five hundred experts were summoned to Washington to "work out" a new system of dispensing health care to the nation.

At first, the names of these experts were not made available. Under pressure, a list of the savants was finally published. But this did little to lift the veil of anonymity. The public still didn't know who they were. The names weren't controversial, because they weren't known. Few could be called famous. No one was elected. No one was accountable. They were "experts."

The problem is self-evident. The New Elite believes that policy can be calibrated. Must be calibrated. There is no other way. The voters and the marketplace are irrelevant to the pursuit. For what is occurring is not the pursuit of social justice. Justice is seen as an insufficiently objective goal—it's inherently related to what people want. Instead, the New Elite is involved in the search for social perfection. And this of course must be left up to the experts.

REJECTION OF VALUES

It's not so much that the New Elite doesn't have values. All people do. But some people—guess who—don't like to acknowledge that anything as subjective as values could possibly affect a public policy decision. To members of the New Elite, it is essential to one's sense of self-identity to believe that their actions are based entirely on reason. You can ratiocinate the answer. If you're smart enough and you assemble all the relevant data, properly weigh all the variables, and then really think it through, the best possible result will emerge.

Of course, this doesn't work. By bizarre coincidence, the experts always come up with policies that reflect their political prejudices. So much for the role of dispassionate analysis.

Much more to the point, values *should* count in the political arena. In fact, that's why we have elections. The campaign is never fought over who has better data. We all have the same data, but we just give it different weight. Elections are really about whose thumb should be on the scale. The New Elite is into deep denial on this score. Its members like to pretend that they check their values at the door and bring only their brains to the table.

President Clinton's administration, far more so even than that of Jimmy Carter, was a valueless administration. Not that it denied all values, but rather it endorsed each one without priority. Clinton was for everything good simultaneously. Saving money is a good, strong value, and so is spending more money on the needy. But very few politicians salute both values in the same program, and only Bill Clinton did so in the same sentence. In health care, he was for reduced costs *and* extended coverage *and* better-quality care and every other value that's attractive. In the budget, at times, he was for reducing the deficit and creating more programs.

Being for everything is much the same as being for nothing. The whole point of government is choosing which values take precedence over others. To pretend that there's no need to choose is to deprive the majority of the chance to advance its own values.

Where there are no values, there is no ideology. The New Elite has no ideology. Its one belief is in itself. If people certified as the brightest are permitted to make all the decisions, everyone will be better off. So it's *wrong* to bring values, or anything else other than the highest possible "competence," into the act. Values, programs, ideology—all those things involve choice. But with the most competent people in charge, we won't have to choose. We can all have it all—just like the new class whose own happy experience has blinded it to the limits on attainable reward.

All of the above explains why President Clinton seemed so inconsistent. On Haiti, on Bosnia, on Somalia, on major appointments, on gays in the military, on a host of issues great and small, he changed his mind, sometimes reversing himself completely. Commentators were amazed at his inconsistency, but seemed puzzled by the reason for it. Many saw it as a character flaw. But it simply stemmed from an absence of values. Inconsistency is inevitable when one prefers competence to ideology. Every change in facts produces a change in policy when that policy isn't rooted in cohesive principle. A balloon will float all over the place if it isn't tied to something.

Clinton was inconsistent because he treated each issue separately. As each problem came up, he assembled the facts and the experts, ingested a staggering amount of information, ratiocinated to beat the band, and then spat out the answer. Then it was on to the next problem. One answer might have no philosophical connection to another.

But it's really not supposed to work that way. It didn't work that way for FDR or Ronald Reagan. They didn't treat each issue as distinct. Every issue that came chugging along on the assembly line got sprayed with the same color paint. Those presidents had certain values and they applied them consistently.

It's not that consistency is the highest possible goal. Facts do change, and leaders must be flexible. But as a general rule, there should be general rules. A leader should believe in certain principles and apply them to the specific issues that arise.

In all fairness to Clinton, the need for consistency in foreign policy was clearer when the cold war was still raging. The existence of one rival superpower simplified our foreign policy goals. The Soviet state had so recently crumbled that new goals and priorities were still being debated. But goals there must be, enabling us to proceed from general principles to particular decisions. To reverse this process is, as Sartre pointed out, immoral.

Inconsistency stems from lack of thought—from a lack of carefully thought-out general principles based on clearly enunciated values. Thought alone won't do it. Values are the essential ingredient, without which policy can no more be formulated than bricks can be made without mortar.

The absence of values is always noticed, but it often looks like something else. In the Carter presidency, some spoke of lack of passion. With Clinton, the verdict was "inconsistency," and one widely reprinted analysis described all the disparate cut-and-run decisions as a form of promiscuity. What does it say about our age that we describe all failures of governance in terms of personal characteristics? Why do we doubt that philosophy, or its lack, can affect what people do—and a thousand times more so than character flaws or quirks? It is a great paradox of our time that the dominance of a new class supposedly based on intelligence has been coincident with an incapacity to take thought seriously.

It must be acknowledged that Clinton was boldly decisive in one area— deficit reduction. Against passionate lobbying from some of his inner circle (Labor Secretary Robert Reich, for one), he finally accepted Alan Greenspan's implied promise that reducing the deficit (raising taxes and cutting spending) would result in lower interest rates, which could lead to economic stimulus. There are learned economists on both sides of this proposition. Some believe that tax cuts, rather than deficit reduction, provide the surer road to economic stimulus. Others point to the astonishing boom of the 1990s as resulting from Clinton's reduction of our vast budget deficit.

But this is not a book about economic policy, about whether Ronald Reagan or Bill Clinton (or George W. Bush) was right. Our concern is with how the electorate responds to new class dominance. And the answer to that is quite clear: the Left Behinds, the majority of the electorate, want policies directed at the common good, rather than at the perceived satisfaction of in- terest groups. The most significant thing about Clinton's economic policy was that he had one. This wasn't a study group, it was a budget—enacted into law. It included a surtax on incomes over $250,000 and the "abolition of welfare as we know it."

Clinton's was a national program in which the rich and the poor were obviously being made to sacrifice for what was hopefully the common good.

Unlike so many of the decisions of the early Clinton years, the economic program was seen as an expression of majoritarian values. Lowering interest rates for the middle class was a value chosen by Clinton as more important than reducing taxes or spending more on social programs. It was an exception to the way the Clinton administration had been perceived, and was to prove an important one.

The absence of values not only makes consistent policies impossible, but it also deprives the majority of choice. If the experts can't understand the fine print of health care reform or arms control, then how can the voters? But everyone understands the values underlying those proposals. If candidates would only proclaim their values rather than hinting at their plans, then the electorate could make rational decisions, and policy would begin in the voting booth.

SYMBOLS OVER SUBSTANCE

When Justice Byron White said he was retiring from the Supreme Court, President Clinton got to make his first appointment to the nation's highest bench. Fifteen years had passed since a Democrat had possessed this opportunity. The waiting list of the party faithful had grown very long. There were many fine names from which to choose. The president finally made an outstanding choice, Ruth Bader Ginsburg. But how he made that choice, and why, tell us how things work after a new class has altered our standards.

At first, the president had decided against naming Judge Ginsburg. Despite her years of advocacy for women's rights and her strong belief that a woman's right to choose an abortion was protected by the federal Constitution, there were those among her fellow feminists who opposed her appointment. They conceded that she supported the landmark abortion rights case of *Roe v. Wade,* but feared that she did so for the wrong reason. She seemed to believe that the right to abortion was guaranteed by the Fourteenth Amendment's requirement of equal rights. *Roe v. Wade* had been decided on other grounds. Justice Harry Blackmun had based his historic decision on the "right to privacy," a right nowhere described within the Constitution.

There is no item higher on the new class agenda than the transfer of decision making from elected legislators to lifetime judges. This transfer of power is greatest, of course, when the judges can ignore the law and look solely to the Constitution—not just at what's *in* the Constitution, but also at what might be *inferred* from it. So when Judge Ginsburg, a strong abortion rights advocate, suggested that *Roe* v. *Wade* was justified by actual constitutional language rather than by a "right" that had never occurred to the framers, she tripped the warning wires of the new class. Bells and sirens clanged and howled. Alarmists rushed to oppose Judge Ginsburg. And well they should have: any Supreme Court justice who likes to base her decisions on what the Constitution says, rather than on what she thinks it should have said, cannot be relied upon to legislate rather than adjudicate. Though she reached the right result, she reached it for reasons other than their own.

Their opposition worked. President Clinton backed away from Judge Ginsburg and began to look seriously at other names. In doing so, he was neither more nor less cowardly than most officeholders today. He was simply recognizing a modern fact of life: the extraordinary power of single-issue groups and of anyone claiming to speak for one. Now that majoritarian, broad-based interest groups have been blown up, it's the splinters from the explosion that do the most damage. No offshoot spokesperson is too remote to be given attention. It's the most passionate, often representing only themselves, who get the sound bites on the evening news. There is no center to balance all the claimants for attention. But, of course, in the end, the president appointed Judge Ginsburg. Why? Because of a slogan.

Senator Daniel Patrick Moynihan was an enthusiastic supporter of his friend Judge Ginsburg. Moynihan phoned the president to promote his candidate. The president was not at all sure. He had heard these negative things about her—about her reasons for supporting *Roe* v. *Wade*. Some women's groups didn't like her. Senator Moynihan knew how to respond. He said that he had heard a speech by Erwin Griswold, former U.S. solicitor general and former dean of the Harvard Law School, in which Griswold had described Judge Ruth Bader Ginsburg as "the Thurgood Marshall of the woman's movement."

That did it. Clinton was entranced. He had what he wanted: a slogan. More than a slogan, a sound bite: "the Thurgood Marshall of the woman's movement." Better yet, "The former dean of the Harvard Law School has called her 'the Thurgood Marshall of the woman's movement.'" And so the appointment was made.

Justice Ginsburg has served on the Supreme Court with very evident integrity, intelligence, and diligence. But that is not why she was nominated by the president. In fact, her integrity is what came very close to preventing her nomination. What saved her was a slogan. A symbol.

The triumph of symbols over substance is perhaps the most striking legacy of the new class. One might think that it would be just the reverse, that the ascendancy of so many bright people would influence public discourse toward more, not less, substance. But what has in fact happened is a shocking change, not only in the quality but in the nature of civic debate. Candidates no longer discuss issues; they promote symbols.

The retreat from substance came about because the New Elite does not really care about issues. It seeks to promote not a philosophy, but simply themselves. Their program is neither more taxation nor less taxation: it is that they themselves should decide what taxes should be, that they themselves know best, can act more rationally, with regard to any issue than can the vast voting public. If you campaign on an issue, you are implicitly ratifying the idea of majority rule, for your issue will only prevail if the majority supports it. By talking about issues, one is saying that the voters are best qualified to decide. But by talking about the candidate's brains rather than his or her ideas, one is removing the voters from the process. The smartest should govern, regardless of their ideas. This is what it means to say that an election should be about competence, not ideology.

But, of course, the voters continue to care about issues, and they do not take kindly to candidates who boast of their own IQs, a most vexing state of affairs to those who scorn issues and seek power. How can you get elected without saying where you stand? So far, at least, the answer is to do so with symbols.

If, for example, your goal is to win elections by attracting enough single-issue groups to simulate (falsely) majority support, you can only do so through symbols. For instance, if one were to campaign directly for the gay vote in a substantive way, one would have to discuss issues—to say what changes in the law one supported. This might be controversial, causing the loss of votes of some nongays, and it would be substantive—it would be admitting that the voters have a right to decide. So, instead, the candidate promises to appoint a gay person to a high position. This symbol shows that candidate is "for" gays, but completely avoids having to discuss a program for gay rights. Thus, each constituency is awarded a symbol, but no specific promises. The goal is to attract without risk enough disparate parts to resemble a majority of the whole. Of course, it doesn't work in the long run—the groups awarded symbols often find that's all they get. But the candidates do get elected.

Nor is it only single-issue groups who are entranced and co-opted by symbols. All issues are reduced to symbols now. Health care certainly is a very broad issue, but when a candidate poses with a sick child, and does nothing else, symbol has displaced program. The same is true of visiting a slum or hugging an AIDS victim or riding along in a patrol car. These are symbolic showings of concern. Genuine concern is a good thing to have, and perhaps even to show, but it is not a substitute for proposing solutions to the problem—and proposing them to the voters.

When members of the Clinton team spoke of their administration as being a permanent campaign, they may well have been thinking of their own reliance on tokenism and symbols. These shorthand signals do indeed belong in a campaign, but they're an excuse for, not an exercise of, government.

It's one thing to sell a judicial appointment on the basis of a slogan. But in today's political world, it's all too often the basis of the appointment itself.

MORAL POSTURING

It is instructive to note that when the Clinton administration raised taxes on high-income earners, many in the White House justified the action not in economic terms but rather as an issue of morality. The 1980s were described as a period of unbridled greed, and the surtax was merely the just reversal of ill-gotten gain. (This rhetoric proved embarrassing when it was learned that Hillary Clinton in the selfsame feverish eighties had made $100,000 from a $1,000 investment in the commodities market.)

The trademark fault of the New Elite is not so much hypocrisy as moral posturing. The reason for the ubiquity of this haughty habit is that it helps to evade majority rule. If something is a moral imperative, we need not wait for it to have majority support. It is easy to understand how this approach gained acceptance during the civil rights struggle and the Vietnam protest—there were real moral imperatives involved there, and the public response seemed maddeningly slow. The New Elite sensed a willingness to bypass or truncate normal legislative processes in deference to the moral fervor of a relative few. So, in time, everything became a moral issue, in the face of which the majority is supposed to shut up.

And, of course, moral superiority follows very naturally from a feeling of intellectual superiority. If one supposes long enough that one thinks better than other people, then it's just one step to the supposition that one feels things better than other people, too, that one has a superior sensitivity to the moral issues of the day. And so when the New Elite (as they so frequently do) use the phrase "This is the moral thing to do," what they really mean is "This is what I want to do." Only those absolutely certain of their certified superiority could actually believe that "moral" is a synonym for "my."

It is difficult to exaggerate how often now the moral card is played. Members of the new class believe that anyone who disagrees with them must either be stupid or corrupt. Without these disabilities, everyone would agree with the new class proposals. So if someone questions some detail in a health care plan, it's either because they don't understand it or because they are looking to make unconscionable profits from a less perfect program.

Most people would rather be called stupid than immoral. It's more galling to have one's motives attacked than one's opinions. Which is why there's so much sardonic celebration when someone who denounces greed is found to have embraced it. The use of moral posturing to preclude debate, because debate assumes majority decisions, is sensed by the public and bitterly resented.

Moral posturing is more than merely irritating. The constant repetition of this theme blunts our senses and makes a truly ethical society less possible. It's like the little boy who cried wolf. There are moral dangers, and alarms that must be sounded, but who will ever hear them amid such constant clamor?

TWELVE

The Revolt of the Left Behinds

So how did Bill Clinton ever get reelected? If he came out of the gate in 1992 as the poster child of the New Elite, then how did he manage to beat that embodiment of the Left Behinds, Bob Dole, in 1996? The answer begins in the remarkably seminal election of 1994.

1994: THE REVOLT BEGINS

As the congressional elections of 1994 grew nearer and nearer, it became increasingly clear that the Republican Party was going to do well. Everyone said so: polls and pols, commentators and columnists, even most Democrats. The signs were, after all, unmistakable—the party opposing the president usually does better in the midterm election; *this* president was spectacularly unpopular; there were many more Democratic incumbents than Republicans on the ballot, so the anti-incumbent feeling of the time, so visible in the term-limit movement, was bound to hurt the president's party.

Which is why everyone said that the Republicans would pick up seats. Some said many seats. Some even spoke of gaining control of the Senate. But no one—absolutely no one—predicted just how total the Republican victory would turn out to be. Both houses of the Congress became Republican for the first time in forty years. Democratic governors of liberal states, tribal monoliths like Mario Cuomo in New York were toppled by relative unknowns. Most significantly, in a year of supposed anti-incumbency, not one single incumbent Republican running for the House, the Senate, or a governorship was defeated.

The dominance of one party was so complete, the change so dramatic, that not only the victors but also many of their foes found the word "revolution" to be appropriate.

It was, in fact, a counterrevolution. What happened so memorably in November 1994 was, more than anything else, simply the Revolt of the Left Behinds. This is not to detract in any way from the very considerable organizational, political, and recruitment skills of the Republican leadership, but the election of 1994 cannot be adequately explained in traditional political terms.

It was partisan, all right. It was the most stunning rejection of the Democrats imaginable. But it was not so much rejection of specific political issues. It was far more a rejection of philosophy. And more than that, a rejection of attitude. And more than that, more than anything else, a rejection of people. It was rejection of dominance by the New Elite.

It is true that the New Elite is more ubiquitous and visible within the Democratic Party than the Republican. But the new class distinction is not really partisan. Most voters in both parties are Left Behinds and neither party has escaped transformation by new class attitudes. The Republican Party recently has been much better at attracting Left Behind voters, but this is not inevitably the case.

We have seen, for example, that the election of Bill Clinton probably would not have occurred had strident demagogues not dominated the rostrum of the Republican national convention. The religious right may be the farthest thing imaginable from the New Elite's legacy, but single-issue politics and moral posturing are not. The public runs from extremism, right or left, because it correctly senses that the real threat to tradition cannot be from the center.

The point is not which party has more members of the New Elite. What the public, which is very smart, really cares about is which party most permits majority rule. It is the simple test, and it is the fulcrum on which each party's fortunes have risen or dropped since the emergence of the New Elite. The question is always the same: who speaks for the majority? And the answer has little to do with issues, but must be sensed instead by an electorate searching for signals. Most people want a signal not even that government respects them, but merely that it knows that they exist. The public is increasingly vigilant about a new class (and therefore anyone else) that thinks it knows best what is good for them.

This is the background of the election of 1994. More dramatically than in any other election in our time (save the Bush/Gore race of 2000), the voters' desperate search for a majoritarianism found sharp focus in a single campaign. Everything came together from both sides to illuminate the threatened value that remained their chief concern. The signals this time seemed remarkably clear.

We begin with the Contract with America. Congressman Newt Gingrich and his allies regarded the Contract as the key to the election. Now let us see.

In September 1994, almost every Republican candidate for the Senate and the House gathered in Washington to sign the Contract. Press releases went out. The network news showed all those candidates linking arms, together. The message was that virtually every one of those Republicans had pledged, if elected, to vote for passage of the same ten things. This was the Contract with America.

At first, this was seen by many as merely a gimmick—that day's sound bite. The polls showed that very few voters had read, or even heard of, the Contract with America.

But it was read very carefully in the White House. The Contract had several parts, of course, but what immediately caught the attention of the young Democratic analysts was the economic part. They cheered, they went wild with glee. Because it seemed obvious to them that this was just restated Reaganomics—reduction of taxes plus balanced budget equals huge increases in the deficit. This was it! A great campaign issue. The Republicans' own Contract could be used to defeat them.

And so the Democrats began talking about the Contract. In fact, they never shut up. They said it was "Reaganomics," and they said this over and over again. They paid to say it, on the air, in commercials, lots of them. It became central to the Democratic congressional campaign.

In every human endeavor, but most particularly in politics, there operates a law of unintended consequences. The unintended consequence of the Democratic attack on the Contract with America was that it nationalized the congressional campaign and became the forerunner of the nationalized congressional campaign orchestrated so successfully by George Bush and Karl Rove in 2002.

This is what proved fatal to the Democrats. It was a case of kamikaze rhetoric. Nothing could have been more harmful to the party of Clinton in 1994 than to nationalize the congressional elections.

"All politics is local," goes the famous saying, inaccurately attributed to Tip O'Neill. The saying is (or, until recently, used to be) quite true. Every two years, the polls and ballots showed, the voters hated the Congress but liked their own member of the House—and voted for that incumbent. This is partly a matter of pork—building dams, keeping open military bases, or in other ways seeming to bring jobs to the district.

But it was something else as well. All politics was local because so little was national. The weakening of political parties and the dominance of single-issue groups that accompanied the rise of the New Elite almost put an end to national political discussion. There was nothing left to keep politicians accountable on issues affecting everyone, and there was every incentive for them to deliver on promises to fragmented sections of the electorate. Politicians still mentioned the broad issues, but were specific only on the narrow ones—telling each disparate group what it wanted to hear.

All this changed in September 1994, when the Democrats decided to run against the Contract with America. This spotlight on the Contract nationalized the election. It emphasized to the voting public that all Republican candidates were running on the same platform. They were all saying the same thing. After decades of New Elite–style politics, this was revolutionary. The entire American electorate was being addressed at the same time, and on all the same issues. Or so it seemed. They were being spoken to as part of a whole, not as members of one interest group or another.

It made all the difference. We have seen how Ronald Reagan's popularity was heavily tied to his seeming to address the whole country at once. Even when people disagreed with specific points of his message, they voted for him because there was a message, seemingly inclusive.

So it was with the Contract with America. The overnight White House polls indicated that most Americans didn't like economic proposals that seemed likely to increase the deficit. The Contract included such proposals. So they attacked the Contract.

This was a terrible mistake. For one thing, most Americans hadn't read, or even heard of, the Contract with America. For many people, the Democratic attack meant only that all Republicans were campaigning on the same set of ideas. This seemed to be a very welcome change. Even people who feared a growth in the deficit tended to welcome the existence of a clear economic platform of which that was a part.

The most attractive thing about the Contract with America was its supposed audience: everybody. The second most attractive feature was what the Contract left out. It said nothing about abortion. It said nothing about school prayer. These omissions were critical. The Republicans had a position on school prayer—they favored it—and their position (unlike that on abortion) was known to be shared by a clear majority of Americans. Even so, if school prayer had been featured as one of the ten points in the Contract, that Contract would have seemed less a majoritarian document. This is because school prayer—like gay rights—is not one of the broad national issues that concern most people most of the time. If it were to become the featured issue, then even people who agreed with the particular position would be uncomfortable; they might sense that single-issue groups were controlling the agenda.

The Contract dealt primarily with economic concerns. When it did include social issues, they were those that bothered most people much of the time—crime and welfare—and were related to economic concerns as well. Some of the economic proposals—such as cutting the capital gains tax—were scarcely high priorities for, or even supported by, a clear majority of the average voters. But they were economic proposals, part of a platform that seemed to address most people's biggest worries. Whether or not they ended up raising the deficit, this time it was the Republicans who were saying, "It's the economy, stupid."

And it was the Republicans, as the Democrats foolishly kept saying, who had an agenda. No wonder the election was so one-sided. The Republicans were running as a party, and the Democrats, fearful of association with an unpopular president, were running as individuals, occasionally attacking the opposition party but never mentioning their own. If voters wanted a coherent set of principles, they were given only one place to look. In a country starved for community, rather than tribalism, the idea of a political party that was broad based, rather than a collection of factions, seemed highly attractive. When there appears to be only one party on the ballot, we should not be so surprised when that party wins.

Still another disastrous feature of the Democratic counterattack was the use of the word "Reaganomics." It is perfectly true that the Contract with America appeared on its surface to threaten the sort of deficit surge that marked the Reagan years. But given the fact that the congressional campaigns had been nationalized, and that the Republicans had a platform and the Democrats did not, the use of the word "Reaganomics," however appropriate, caused many voters to visualize the contest in terms of one of the most popular former presidents against an incumbent whose poll numbers after two very bad years had tanked. A referendum pitting Reagan against Clinton was not a tactic that the Democratic strategists, upon reflection, should have employed.

The 1994 election, like every other election since the growth of the New Elite, was a quest by the voters for majoritarianism, a fight against the fragmentation of our society. What was unusual about 1994 was how extraordinarily clear for once the signposts of that quest seemed to be.

First, there was the Contract with America and, far more significantly, the response to it, which signaled repeatedly that the sense of community people sought was offered only by one side.

Second, there was Clinton himself. With or without comparison to Reagan, President Clinton had become in many minds the embodiment of the New Elite. If diabolical programmers of Manchurian Candidates had worked their mischief for decades, they could not in their wildest disabling fantasies have hoped to produce an administration sending so many alarming signals to the Left Behinds as that of President Clinton. The health care fiasco alone wins the Order of Pavlov Award for striking instant fear and rage in the hearts of those tormented by an elite whose central belief is that it alone knows what is best for the governed. The first two years of Bill Clinton's first term were virtually a parody of what it was to be governed by the New Elite.

There is a third factor as well in the outcome of the 1994 elections. It reflects just as strongly as the others how the New Elite has transformed our political landscape—and how counterproductively for itself. This third factor is gerrymandering. Or to be more specific, gerrymandering to achieve specific racial results.

The New Elite hates the idea of majority rule. The basis of this hatred is its own sense of superiority. If its members supposedly have been proven to be smarter than everyone else, then why should they be denied the power to govern merely because there are so many more people on the other side? It becomes important—indeed, nothing could be more important—to dismantle the structures and discredit the idea of majority rule.

One way of doing so is to say that each different group in America should be allowed to govern itself. The unexamined assumption of this outrageous new tribalism is that a nation is only a collection of groups, not an entity unto itself. It is a way of saying that Americans should be defined by their differences rather than by what they have in common.

The exceptionally controversial book *The Bell Curve*, by Richard Herrnstein and Charles Murray, speaks approvingly of a new IQ class, which the authors call the "Cognitive Elite." It is a class virtually identical to the New Elite described in this book, though Herrnstein and Murray spend most of their time "proving" that the Cognitive Elite is really smarter and scarcely discussing the social and political ramifications of the new class. One of their few forays into this arena is the brief suggestion that all the different "clans" in America should live exclusively with one another and, to a large extent, be governed by themselves.

Have we not heard this before? Yes, we have. The call for separatism as an alternative to majority rule was advocated by President Clinton's nominee for assistant attorney general for civil rights—Lani Guinier. And when her position on this matter had begun to be widely publicized, Clinton withdrew her name.

What do Charles Murray and Lani Guinier have in common? Plenty: contempt for the majority and consequent advocacy of separatism. Though one has been called a racist and the other a civil rights leader, though one is a hero to the far right and the other to the far left, these two academic stars— one a Ph.D. from M.I.T. and the other a J.D. from Yale—share an outlook more significant than placement on the political spectrum: lack of trust in the majority and a desire to fragment the nation, by defining and segregating each human being in terms of clan or color.

One way to do this is by gerrymandering. There is nothing new about the practice of drawing the lines of legislative or congressional districts to achieve a specific result. Its goal traditionally has been political, and it was a very common practice: if you deliberately draw the lines of a district to include a clear majority of, say, Democrats, then the district will always vote Democratic. The Republicans, of course, did the same thing. Everybody in politics did. Only they didn't admit it, because they knew that fixing an election was wrong.

In 1982, this changed in two ways. First, it was no longer a secret. In fact, it was a law. Congress amended the Voting Rights Act to require gerrymandering in certain cases. Second, those certain cases were not political. They were racial. The congressional amendment required that African Americans and other minorities be given an enhanced opportunity to elect one of their own to Congress and to state legislatures.

At first, the effects were not clear. We had to wait for the census in 1990 before any congressional lines could be redrawn.

And then they were. In the South, the process of creating new districts was particularly interesting. Two groups were working side by side to make sure that the 1982 amendment to the Voting Rights Act was strictly enforced. Both groups joined in insisting that new districts be created in which the majority of voters would be African Americans. The first group pushing for this result included a number of African American congressional leaders. The second group was the Republican National Committee.

Amazingly, the first group didn't ask what the second group was doing there. It is easy to see the motives of the first group. African American leaders wanted to elect more blacks to Congress. This is perfectly understandable, particularly in the South, where even the ablest African American candidates had often found it difficult, solely because of their race, to attract white voters. In other words, African Americans were motivated by their past.

The Republicans were motivated by their future. They were aware of a fundamental law of physics: the more water that is poured into a glass, the less there remains in the pitcher. The glass in this case was each new African American–majority congressional district. The water was the Democratic voters. The pitcher was the state.

Let us say that half the voters in a state are Democrats and the other half are Republicans. The state has five congressional districts. The census results require that new district lines be drawn. Those in charge of doing so could create five new districts, in each of which African Americans were 20 percent of the electorate (the African American percentage of the state population). Instead, they were urged to create one district that was 80 percent African American. The remaining four districts would each therefore contain an electorate of which no more than 5 percent was African American.

This would indeed result in the election of an African American member of Congress, which perhaps before that would have been unlikely. And that was and remains a worthy goal. Ours is a representative democracy, and it is undesirable that some groups should be underrepresented because of bigotry.

But the manner in which this worthy goal was achieved proved counterproductive. Every election analysis shows that African Americans vote overwhelmingly Democratic. So when one puts most of the African Americans into one district, one is moving mostly Democrats into that district, too. Which means that one is moving Democrats out of the surrounding districts. Which means that those districts are more likely to vote Republican.

And that is exactly what happened. In its comprehensive analysis of the 1994 election, on the Sunday following that election, the *New York Times,* in an article titled "Did Racial Redistricting Undermine Democrats?" said,

> Some scholars and political analysts say that the creation of majority African American districts in 1990 may have played an important role in costing the Democrats control of the House of Representatives. They estimate that the Democrats may have lost ten seats this year, mainly in the South, because of redistricting, on top of the five seats they feel were lost in 1992.
>
> They argue that reapportionment not only siphoned solid Democratic votes from white districts, but also helped Republicans attract higher-caliber candidates and raise more money by giving them a better shot at winning those districts. In addition, when African American voters were removed from marginally Republican districts, the Democrats' chances of winning such seats became that much slimmer.

"There is absolutely no secret that the South on a Congressional-district-by-Congressional-district basis got more Republicans in total because of minority districts," said an official with the Democratic Congressional Campaign Committee who would speak only on the condition of not being identified.

When asked about the likelihood of the Supreme Court declaring African American–majority districts unconstitutional, the chief counsel of the Republican National Committee was quoted as saying, "Look at the results. We'd be nuts to want to see those districts abolished."

Far be it for this book to suggest which party will most benefit African Americans. That decision is up to each voter. But African Americans vote so overwhelmingly Democratic that their decision in this matter at this time is clear. That being so, how can the creation of African American–majority districts possibly be seen as other than a disaster for African American voters? As a result of the 1994 election and the consequent Republican takeover, members of the Congressional Black Caucus lost the chairmanships of three committees and seventeen subcommittees in the Congress.

It is hard to believe that something as foolhardy as the 1982 amendment to the Voting Rights Act would have been supported by the average African American voter. And perhaps it was not. Much of its support came from whites who wanted to help send more African Americans to Congress but, having no faith whatsoever in majority rule, came up with a way to subvert it. Are African Americans better or worse off today in terms of congressional power than before the amendment went into effect? Were those manipulators of our rules correct to believe that no white majority will ever elect an African American candidate? Perhaps not: in the 1996 presidential preference polls, the most popular potential candidate was General Colin Powell.

The election of 1994 was the Revolt of the Left Behinds. Its three determining factors—the unpopularity of President Clinton, the nationalization of the race by the Republicans, and the gerrymandering of southern congressional districts—are all manifestations of the transformation of our politics by the New Elite. Campaigns today are fought over symbols, not issues, and the symbols that gather the most votes are those that seem aimed not at factions but at everyone. And when those who are unwilling or unable to signal to everyone start tampering with the rules in order to avoid majority rule, the results are likely to be very different from those intended. The roots of democracy are sufficiently deep that the hardy plant can withstand defoliants and pruning. While the tendrils will creep up in unexpected places, perhaps cling to the wrong wall, they will grow, eventually upward, nourished by the rich soil of memory and the warm sun of hope.

This point was missed by virtually every commentator who couldn't understand why the election of 1994 turned out the way it did. And at the base of this disbelief was the refusal to acknowledge that most voters really do know what they are doing. The electorate may be imperfectly informed about what or whom they voted for, but it's very hard to argue that they didn't feel strongly about what they were voting against.

The New Elite never got it, either. When one loses an election, the reasonable question is "What did we do wrong?" and not "What did the voters do wrong?"

All too many were asking this absurd question. The *New Yorker,* commenting on the 1994 election, said, "Disappointed Election Night commentators tied themselves into knots to explain away the massive repudiation. . . . [U]nderneath these rationalizations, you know they really wanted to shout simply, 'The people are wrong!' But our populist political culture does not permit blaming the people." ABC's Peter Jennings said in a radio commentary that "it's clear that anger controls the child and not the other way around. . . . [T]he voters had a temper tantrum . . . [and] the nation can't be run by an angry two-year old." The *New York Times'* major editorial on the subject, defending the counterculture against attack by Newt Gingrich, actually asked, "Would many Americans truly like to imagine a society returned to the dictatorship of the majority culture?"

And there you have it. One cannot understand, let alone reverse, the results of an election if one sees the majority as the enemy—and a stupid enemy at that. The election of 1994 was primarily over the fact that the majority is tired of being treated like an enemy. To know that is to be able to move forward. And what direction constitutes forward—left or right or closer to the center—will and should be determined by the voters. Those who think they know best what that direction should be have the duty to persuade, and not deride, the multitudes whom we must see not as our enemy but as ourselves.

THE DEATH OF ROBESPIERRE: THE COUNTER COUNTERREVOLUTION OF 1996

The Republicans' victory of 1994 was so striking that almost everyone used the same word: *revolution*. It wasn't just a changing of the guard—it was a storming of the Bastille.

The leader of the revolt was unquestionably Newt Gingrich, the new speaker of the House. He strode through the Capitol as if it were conquered territory. From the very start, he was highly controversial. To some he was Spartacus, to others Robespierre. As it turned out, the case for Spartacus was limited to only two similarities—Gingrich lost his battle, and he was crucified. The latter is, of course, a metaphor, but none other will do. Gingrich quickly surpassed Bill Clinton as the object of widespread scorn. His extraordinary unpopularity was a major reason why the once unpopular Clinton was able to be handily reelected president in 1996.

How could this be? Wasn't Newt Gingrich the champion of traditional moral values? Wasn't this conservative Georgia congressman a typical Left Behind? The answers to these two questions are (a) yes and (b) no.

Newt Gingrich is dramatic proof that you don't have to be politically liberal to be seen as a member of the New Elite. His rise, and almost immediate fall, show us how little new class politics has to do with being "liberal" or "conservative." The real issue is no issue—it's who you are, not what your program is.

Who, then, was Newt Gingrich? He was a Ph.D. marked by impatience, incivility, and unmistakable moral fervor. This, more than his program, is what did him in: embodying characteristics of the new class—the class that voters only sense but still deplore.

In the prestigious *Almanac of American Politics*, its editor, Michael Barone, a conservative, attributes Gingrich's unpopularity in part to press bias, but concedes that Gingrich was characterized by "a cocksureness, professional abstractness about policy, a more than occasional petulance of high self-regard." And this is from his *defender*. Barone's words are a perfect description of New Elite attitude. Gingrich was the teacher whom every student hated—always right, morally smug, deaf to anyone's argument but his own. By comparison, he made Bill Clinton look quiet and conciliatory.

In addition to embodying the least attractive elements of the New Elite persona, Gingrich made a huge tactical error. He shut down the government. While Clinton and Gingrich had been playing chicken with the federal budget, both cars went over the cliff. Without a new appropriations bill, there was no money; consequently, much of the government closed down.

Gingrich was blamed. Many conservatives thought that Clinton should have been the bad guy, because he was the one who had vetoed the appropriations bills. But the public ascribed the blame to Gingrich. This is instructive.

Shutting down the government rather than compromising "professional abstractions about policy" is exactly the sort of thing that a New Elite fanatic would do. The New Elite does not believe in compromise, regardless of the consequences of intransigence. Compromise is for those who aren't sure that they are absolutely right.

Compromise is also for those who want to be reelected. And in this regard Clinton was very far removed from the New Elite. The president whose first two years were a textbook case on how to offend the electorate ended up beating Bob Dole by eight percentage points. Clinton, who had received only 43 percent of the vote in 1992 (when Perot was a factor) achieved 49 percent in 1996, with Perot still in the race. What had changed?

Clinton had changed. Jimmy Carter had been much more of a New Elite president than Clinton. Carter stuck to his guns, and he lost. Clinton was adaptable, and he won. When cornered, Clinton made a chameleon seem constant. One of the reasons Clinton was never a pure example of the New Elite lay in his skill as a political magician. He could turn on a dime. (And he could turn on a friend.) Call it shameless opportunism or heeding the people's voice, he knew what people wanted and he gave it. His enemies called him the world's best snake-oil salesman, but that was the secret of his survival. His hands were quicker than the eye and his footwork was phenomenal. All things considered, the case can be made that Bill Clinton was a New Elite president only from the neck up.

Clinton got out ahead of Spartacus's mob and started leading the charge. He announced in his state of the union speech that "the era of big government is over." And in August 1996, with the national election upon him, he signed the bill eliminating federal welfare. Many of his friends were aghast, and some even resigned their federal posts as a matter of principle. But the electorate responded with a landslide.

There was one more factor that ensured Clinton's reelection. In 1995, the Oklahoma City federal building was bombed by fanatics, with terrible loss of life. Clinton spoke to the country, and spoke very well. It is impossible to avoid comparing the incident with George W. Bush's remarks at the World Trade Center site, six years later. But the events of 9/11, still so vivid at the time of this writing, should not obscure the national impact of the earlier attack. The whole country was stricken. At a stage in history when national purpose was unclear and unity unraveled, a sense of community and purpose was suddenly restored. Any president who took the microphone at such a time would have won high approval, but to have used the moment well, both in Oklahoma City and New York, to speak not only to but for the nation, was to be given some measure of immunity from the fractious disparagements of class-riven warfare.

It isn't that war on terrorism trumps all other issues. It's that community trumps disunity in a country too long fragmented. A common foe provides a common identity, and a leader who speaks to that commonality can attract the respect, if not always the votes, of that newly unified whole.

Our society has been fragmented for so long that those associated with its renewal are rewarded not just with Teflon but with armor.

THIRTEEN

Thong with the Wind:
The Clinton Impeachment Drama

Do you suppose Newt Gingrich *did* know what he was doing when he shut down the government? The shutdown effectively may have ended his career, but it almost had the same effect on that of his archfoe, President Clinton.

Though in a very roundabout way. When the government closed down, many federal employees temporarily disappeared. They weren't being paid, and they didn't come to work. Even the White House was deprived of staff. All of a sudden, all the gofers were gone. But someone remembered that White House interns were not civil service employees and therefore were unaffected by the shutdown. So the interns were drafted into unaccustomed service.

One of them, Monica Lewinsky, a young woman from California, was asked to deliver a pizza to the late-working president, who was alone in the Oval Office. This she did. Only a few minutes together, but that was enough. The government shutdown soon ended, and it would shrink to a historical footnote compared with the story of the couple whom it had inadvertently brought together.

And what a story it was. Future generations who didn't live through it would scarcely be expected to believe the degree to which it dominated the news. There was no other subject. This was true from the moment the story broke, like a scene from a Fellini film, though even Fellini might have thought it a little over the top. The Pope was visiting Cuba. He was about to share a stage with Fidel Castro. The entire American press corps was crowding around the stage. Anchors were jostling for the best position. There were enough cameras to film *The Lord of the Rings*.

Then all of a sudden The Story broke. People crammed the communication trailers to hear the excited voices of their Washington colleagues: The President and the Intern! There was proof! Playing around in the Oval Office!

Neither the Pope nor the Supreme Leader had a chance. All they saw were reporters' backs, as the entire journalistic mob turned and fled toward the mainland, in every heart the quest to homestake The Story first. As network jets roared upward and neophyte stringers took up abandoned microphones, it must have seemed to Castro much like that happy moment four decades earlier when all the Batistas rushed to their escape. God knows what the Pope was thinking.

Once ensconced back in their studios, the telegenic punditry pulled out all the stops. The view was nearly unanimous that this was one of the major stories of all time. It was portentously proclaimed a "constitutional crisis." Soon it was a given that the president's days in office were numbered, and that those numbers didn't go very high. Just one more smoking gun—though that metaphor from an earlier constitutional crisis now surely could be improved upon—and Clinton would be driven from office. With each new prurient detail, none of which was withheld from public gaze, the removal of the president from office seemed more certain.

The sordid details continued to be publicly disclosed, with such specificity as to render most school sex education classes redundant—any fourth grader was now qualified to teach them, simply by having watched the evening news.

A special prosecutor was appointed. The Articles of Impeachment were drawn. The pundits now debated mostly when, not if, the president would be forced out and whether he would go to prison. Even the president's defenders described his actions in terms and tones originally launched in Salem. When the special prosecutor finally issued his report, this bulging and salacious tome seemed very like the sort of thing that used to be confiscated at customs.

Of course, the reader knows how this drama played out. The president was not removed from office. The votes against him were largely partisan and not enough. President Clinton served out his complete term, right up to the final pardon. But in the meantime, something remarkable happened. The longer the impeachment proceedings went on, the more prurient or disgusting the details revealed, the more hysterically the president was vilified, the more popular he became. Well, "popular" is not quite right—people on both sides of the impeachment issue were either cracking jokes or fuming with rage. Bill Clinton was not "popular" if that means what people thought of his character.

But the longer the scandal went on, the greater his public support became. People did not want him to be forced out of office. Whatever people thought of his personal life, they increasingly approved of his performance as president. The more virulent the attacks, the more damning the evidence, the higher his approval rating grew.

Why was this? The answer to that question is a major point of this book. It is that people are often smart and experts sometimes fools. The public did not approve of Clinton's personal misconduct. Most were disgusted with his character and judgment. But they knew that he had been reelected president by a landslide.

Clinton had been the clear choice of a substantial plurality of the voters. To remove him from office would be *to nullify an election.* That's the real point: the clear will of the majority must never be set aside, except on solid constitutional grounds. The janitor in the Senate hallway knew instinctively and far better than the fulminators in the chamber that high crimes and misdemeanors do not include oral sex.

Clinton's growing popularity when threatened with removal by impeachment can be best understood in the context of New Elite mischief. For many decades, the voters' will as expressed at the polls often had been struck down by rulings and decrees out of reach of the electorate. Our society had been significantly reconstructed in both rules and attitudes so as to remove much decision making from even the remote control of the voters. The things that people voted for were not the things that seemed to happen. The people whom people voted in were not the ones who seemed really to be in charge. There were all sorts of rules and requirements and regulations that often seemed like nonsense, but there was no complaint department, not even the ballot box. Who was in charge? It was hard to tell.

The rule of law is indeed the brightest gem in liberty's crown and America's greatest gift by example to the world. But the reason that law should rule is that it has been passed with the consent of the governed. When that ceases to be true, and also when people cease to believe that it is true, then law seems not to rule but merely to coerce.

In our highly complex society, laws are often lengthy and difficult to understand. They sometimes create bureaucracies to implement the law, through rules and regulations of their own. And sooner or later a citizen is told to do something, or not to do something, that can't possibly be what the voters had in mind. This has nothing to do with constitutional rights, which are and should be above the law and which protect speech and actions that are often very unpopular. If they weren't unpopular, they wouldn't need protection. But just because there are some inviolable rights doesn't mean that lawmakers and voters should be divorced. If people feel that laws are merely preambles to endless regulations, and that the Constitution is being used not to protect rights but rather to foment more rules without any pretext of legislation, then people will react accordingly. The will to self-governance is so strong in this country that damming it will only cause eruptions in ways less channeled or reliable than those of representative democracy.

California provides a good example. The voters of California had so little faith in their lawmakers that they started passing statewide referenda in self-defense. The referendum is a very clumsy axe with which to attempt surgery. Originally, it was a populist response to legislatures isolated from the public will by bribery. And now the legislature seemed to have sold out to the single-issue factions whose currency was endorsement without which the politicians' names would not even be on the ballot. So, desperately, like pulling the emergency cord on a runaway train, the California voters froze their property taxes. They cut back funding for what had been the pride of America's public higher education systems. Though most of them believed in diversity (and were, themselves, diverse), they forbade the use of race as a factor in college admission. It is bad to govern by referenda, but tragic to have no alternatives.

The people of America have come to fear the laws passed in their name. So much so that they've even stopped supporting the causes they believe in. This is why a nation overwhelmingly in favor of equal rights for women refused to pass an Equal Rights Amendment to the federal Constitution. They were afraid of the fine print, because they didn't know who would be writing it.

What the voters want is to make the decisions themselves, and the right to change those decisions over time. They want laws that can be changed as people's opinions, or circumstances, change. That's why, when George W. Bush came out in favor of a constitutional amendment banning gay marriage, the polls showed that while a majority of Americans opposed gay marriage, a majority also opposed the amendment. People want things decided neither by the courts nor by amendments, but by ballots.

All of this helps to explain why Clinton's approval ratings rose throughout the impeachment proceedings. The public, justly suspicious of the legalization of formerly private matters, deeply distrustful of constitutional convolutions designed to evade the common will, seeing themselves as rubes in a carnival shell game in which the disappearing coin is majority rule, were smarter than the con men thought. They were willing to accept a great deal of unauthorized change, but throwing an elected president out of office was something else entirely. It took a very long time for the public to feel that even Nixon should go, and he had been playing around not with an intern but with a government. In the matter of the Clinton impeachment, when the network anchors said "constitutional crisis," they were thinking of higher ratings; when the citizens heard the phrase "constitutional crisis," they actually thought about it.

And what they thought was this: if you can remove a president from office because of adultery, or even because he had lied about his adultery, then soon any excuse would do. Any party with enough votes in the Senate could get rid of any president it didn't like. And that's not what the Constitution says. The public, not Ken Starr, was attempting to uphold the rule of law. People who couldn't pronounce *coup d'état* knew one when they saw it.

No, neither Ken Starr nor any of the indignant (and sometimes adulterous) congressmen who backed him up were members of the New Elite. But they were acting as if they were. They were trying to do what the New Elite has been getting away with for so long—bypassing an electoral mandate with "special" prosecutors and rules and pseudolegal smoke and mirrors. The players were different (Hillary Clinton had worked for the House Judiciary Committee at the time of the Nixon impeachment), but the tactic was the same, if not writ large. The removal of a president on such grounds was so obviously contrary to the idea of even having an election that the public just refused to go along.

And that made all the difference. Popular opposition to the removal of an unpopular president caused the impeachment tide to recede. With representative government made unrepresentative through the capture of the parties by single-issue zealots, the last working vestige of majority rule seems to be the public opinion polls. A megaphone is better than a gag, but Madison had something better yet in mind.

FOURTEEN

The Emerging Majority Is the Majority: The Election of 2002

This is not a book about politics. It is the story of a new class and the class war, the uncivil war, that accompanied its rise.

Elections are to some extent a reflection of the progress of this warfare, but which party wins or loses is of far less importance than the transformation of our retreat from the practice of majority rule. Both parties, indeed, all our lives, already have been altered by what is happening—and very much for the worst.

The election map, the Red and the Blue, is merely a thermometer. It is not the illness itself. But to address that illness, it helps to begin by taking one's temperature.

What is going to happen in the new class war? The most recent election provides one answer.

We have seen that every national election is decided in significant part by the backlash against the New Elite. Sometimes that backlash can hurt the Republicans (as in the public rejection of the Newt Gingrich program), but more often it hurts the Democrats, as in the midterm election of 2002.

That election wasn't *supposed* to hurt the Democrats. It was supposed to *help* them—to sweep them into solid control of both the House and the Senate. And this was a very reasonable expectation. George Bush had been elected president in 2000 by a margin so thin and controversial that the winner had to be proclaimed by the U.S. Supreme Court. Squeaky victories are never mandates, but Bush's narrow win was even less auspicious because the courts had been involved. The public, that is to say the Left Behinds, has grown exceptionally wary of political decisions made by unelected judges who serve for life, and the most political decision of all would seem to be the outcome of an election. George Bush received just enough votes to win because he was perceived as a

Left Behind and Gore the poster child of the New Elite. (Of course, Ralph Nader did his part.) In the present climate of public distrust, had the judicial vote been five to four for Gore instead of Bush, the declared winner would have had enormous difficulty establishing his political legitimacy. As it was, even Bush, the putative Left Behind, began his term with a Vesuvian cloud over his head.

His perception by the public changed, of course, within a few days of 9/11. It changed at the moment the president stood atop the rubble of the World Trade Center and told the construction workers that he could hear them just fine and so could the world. His approval ratings soared to exceptional heights. The war in Afghanistan rallied people from every point on the political spectrum to support their commander in chief. The president's rigid adherence to stated principles won further respect, even from some who disagreed with his views.

So why did everyone think that the midterm election of 2002 looked good for the Democrats? The usual answer was that "it's the economy, stupid." And, indeed, the stock market had tanked. It had erased seven trillion dollars of wealth, every nickel of which was lost after Bush took office. Retirement accounts sank to levels that produced great and widespread pain. There was crisis and panic in millions of homes. And no one was sure whether things would get better or worse.

And in this climate of painful retrenchment, the president was proposing a tax cut whose immediate benefit would be most enjoyed by the upper 1 percent of taxpayers. Moreover, he also was backing a total repeal of the federal estate tax, though it seemed that only about four thousand families, most of great wealth, would enjoy the benefit. The president who won because he wasn't of the New Elite now seemed awfully cozy with the old elite, a group no more widely beloved than the IQ meritocracy.

And then, of course, there were the corporate scandals. Enron was the first, and the splashiest, and it was in oil and in Texas. The Bush administration was filled with Texas oilmen, starting with the president and vice president. (Cheney had had to reestablish Wyoming residency because the Constitution forbade the POTUS and veep from being from the same state.) It was not surprising that a Republican administration had a great many former business leaders in its highest posts, but this unexceptional state of affairs became the focus of controversy when the comforting mists of corporate infallibility were dispelled by repeated scandals. Whether or not the Bushies had actually been involved in these headlined misdeeds, they had come from the same world as the miscreants. They had actually *known* some of those handcuffed guys in the orange jumpsuits. Public anger at corporate greed, fueled by a decimated stock market, did not portend a gentle fate for Republican candidates in the off-year election.

Nor was Iraq a perfect way to change the subject. Afghanistan had been one thing. We were clearly after Osama bin Laden, the man who had murdered thousands of innocent Americans. Public support was wide and deep. And the war seemed to go well. Though bin Laden had apparently escaped either capture or death, his organization was badly damaged, its leaders captured or killed or in flight. This war against Al Qaeda seemed as justified as our response to Pearl Harbor.

Saddam Hussein was another thing. Though clearly he was cruel and evil, a torturer of children and the attempted assassin of the first President Bush, there were many who thought that all-out war to change his regime was going too far. What had he done bad *lately*? The extent of his sinister stockpile was debatable, and debated. Further, war against an Arab state in a region and at a moment of spectacular volatility was clearly a very high-stakes risk. The law of unintended consequences had seldom been so greatly leveraged. And the fact that prior to the 2002 election the United States had not yet achieved UN support for its Iraq policy caused great concern among many Americans who thought that in this matter their country should not act alone.

Nor did history enhance Republican hopes as November grew nearer. The party of the incumbent president was *supposed* to lose seats in the off-year elections. It had been that way as far back as almost anyone could remember. The last time that president's party had picked up seats in both chambers two years into his first term was 1934, and the president was FDR. The party that wins the presidency usually sees the tide go out just two years later—and not only in the Congress. The same dynamic applies to governorships and state legislatures. If the pendulum swung back now as it had reliably for sixty-eight years, the Republicans were facing losses.

And as if all of this were not enough to give bounce to the Democratic step, there was also The Book. Everyone in Washington was reading it. *Believing* it. Even George F. Will devoted a *Newsweek* column to his anxiety over what this new text had to say.

The (now) unfortunate name of the book was *The Emerging Democratic Majority.* It was written by John B. Judis and Ruy Teixeira, who are, like the book that they produced, highly intelligent, admirably lucid, and gifted in the assemblage of data. The message of the book is that the Republicans are doomed, in large part because of what the authors call the professional class, the growing number of those who produce ideas, words, and services, rather than products. This new class, together with the growth of black, Asian, and Hispanic populations, labor, and the very large number of women voters concerned with preserving abortion rights, would soon make the Democrats unbeatable.

The numbers did seem to add up. Everyone went crazy, one party with fear and the other with joy. The thesis was so reasonable, so well documented, it *had* to be true. E. J. Dionne spoke for many: "Way before this book appeared in print, early drafts circulated from hand to hand around Washington, provoking debate, controversy, surprise, and—yes—reasoned discussion. Democrats will take heart from its message. Republicans need to know the dangers they face."

The dangers faced by the Republicans were demographic. The groups that had traditionally supported the Democrats were growing as a percentage of the voting population. But the key to the Judis/Teixeira thesis was a group not known as traditional Democrats: the professional class.

This was a major insight, and, as far as it goes, correct. There is indeed a new class of well-educated people. And it is growing. And it is transforming the electoral map. The composition of the new class—Judis and Teixeira call it the "post–New Deal liberal Democrats"—is not identical to the New Elite, but it is close enough. There are significant similarities, and these similarities are enough to prove the authors wrong. A new class *is* growing, but the backlash against it is growing, too, and potentially involves a larger number of voters.

Neither Judis nor Teixeira sees it this way. They do a very good job of describing the direct political impact of the new class, but seemingly ignore any reaction to it. That impact, as they describe it, is indeed significant. They describe the class of higher-skilled professionals as "a group that includes architects, engineers, scientists, computer analysts, lawyers, physicians, registered nurses, teachers, social workers, therapists, designers, interior decorators, graphic artists, and actors." This group, once said to be reliably Republican (actors!), now composes, according to the authors, "21 percent of the voting electorate nationally and are likely near one-quarter in many Northeastern and Far Western States." And these percentages will grow. "Among the professions expected to increase by more than 20 percent [from 1998 to 2008] are a startling combination of jobs that didn't exist or were of marginal significance in the industrial age: actors, directors, and producers, artists and commercial artists, designers and interior designers, camera operators, public relations specialists, counselors, registered nurses, therapists, coaches, special education teachers, preschool teachers, social workers, electrical and electronics engineers, architects and surveyors, agricultural and food scientists, conservation scientists and foresters, medical scientists, computer systems analysts, computer scientists and engineers, physicists and astronomers, and directors of religious activities."

This is the core of their thesis. The new class is the blue in the electoral maps of the Red and the Blue. Just add in voters from among people of color, laborers, and women's rights advocates, and voila! You can't lose.

Except that you did. The midterm election of 2002 was an astonishing victory for the Republican Party. By historical standards, Republicans should have lost twenty-two seats in the House and two in the Senate. Instead, they actually gained seats in both chambers, regaining control of the Senate and strengthening their control of the House.

It is true that many of the elections were very close. A switch of 150,000 votes would have kept Democrats in control of the Senate. (The *New York Times* actually ran a postelection editorial, painfully quizzical in tone, that wondered why so much power should change through so few votes. While cynics might wonder whether the *Times* would have so agonized had the thin margin favored the other party, the same answer would be true in either case: it's the voters, stupid. The way it works, see, is that the candidate with the most votes wins. Close, but many cigars.)

And the election really wasn't close at all: thirty-four million votes in the congressional races were cast for Republicans and only thirty-one million for Democrats. In the state legislatures, where the president's party usually loses about three hundred fifty seats around the country in the midterm election, the Republicans increased their share by two hundred. The emerging majority surely looked more Republican than Democratic.

In fairness to Judis and Teixeira, their book took a pass at the 2002 election. They correctly saw that "a continuing public preoccupation with national security will certainly benefit the Republicans . . . and at least mitigate whatever gains the Democrats had expected." They should have stopped there. But perhaps carried away by the heat of the campaign, Judis threw caution to the winds and on the eve of the election, wrote an article for the October 28 issue of the *New Republic* called "Poll Vault, How the Democrats Could Win." Not win in the long run—win in the coming week. "There are indicators," he wrote, "that the Democrats are running even or slightly ahead. . . . [O]ne of the parties might get swept this November, but it is not likely to be the Democrats."

When the returns were in, there was some explaining to do. Judis followed up with another piece in the *New Republic* that concluded that "although it wasn't apparent until the final days of the election, the Republicans were borne to victory this fall by Bush's energetic response to Osama bin Laden. And there was probably nothing that the Democrats could have done to stop them."

This last sentence is the key to what is going on. Judis's article is even titled "No Fault." There was nothing that the Democrats could do.

If so, that is fortunate, because the general consensus is that the Democrats did in fact do nothing. They waged no campaign. Few raised any issues, and when they did their points were quibbles. There was no real attack on tax policy said to favor the very rich. There was no coordinated effort to tie corporate scandals to many in the administration. (Such as Harvey Pitt—the Securities and Exchange commissioner who quietly quit on election eve.) There was very little said about the proposed war in Iraq. In fact, the only Democratic senator in a tight race who actually voted against authorizing the president to invade Iraq was Paul Wellstone (about whom more below). The oldest and perhaps still largest political party in the world seemed to be waging a major battle for control of the U.S. government under the single banner of prescription drugs. Of course, it lost. Even ailing seniors must have suspected that there might be some other issues around.

Virtually every pundit on every point on the political spectrum agreed on the cause of the Democrats' defeat: they hadn't campaigned on the issues. Aha. But *why* hadn't they campaigned on the issues? That's the real question that reveals the new class role in the way the election went.

Judis and Teixeira were right enough about there being a new professional class. And right in saying that it was going to make all the difference in elections. They just didn't know that that difference would result in *losing* elections, not winning them.

To understand how this works is to understand the character and the menace (to democracy) of the New Elite. Just look.

The first reason that issues no longer matter to the New Elite was expressed with breathtaking candor many years ago by Michael Dukakis, a platinum card member of the new class who, as previously noted, actually ran for president with the boast "This election is about competence, not ideology." Get that? This is why Republicans win. Because the average person, regardless of test scores, is smart enough to know what Dukakis meant, even if the candidate did not.

Not that every Democrat is a member of the New Elite. Far from it. But most of the professional campaign strategists, the summas who want to be sumos, very likely are—and in both parties. (Bush apparently ignores them.) And the New Elite goes well beyond paid advisers. It's the hive that starts the buzz that makes the conventional wisdom so conventional.

That hive believes that most people are too stupid to understand the issues. It's all right to scare old folks about the cost of prescription drugs, but beyond that, forget it. Abolishing the estate tax isn't a concept that most people can grasp—so just leave it alone. Leave every issue alone. Just campaign on being the smartest person there is—certified as the most qualified to solve any issue that does or will arise.

If you believe this, and are also deluded enough to believe that the public agrees with your idiocy, then campaign as Dukakis did, by going around saying "Mirror, mirror, on the wall, who's the smartest one of all? Why it's me! Just send me those issues!"

So when these candidates who followed this advice went on the campaign trail in the portentous summer of 2002, they did not *debate* the issues. They did not *explain* the issues. They *mentioned* the issues.

There were thirty-second TV spots produced, and run at staggering cost, that just showed writing on the screen. Words. These were known as "issue ads." What they did was *list* the issues. White letters on black background. The first word would be PEOPLE. The next was probably SENIORS. Then KIDS. Next, just maybe, for those on the cutting edge of risk, HEALTH CARE, even TAXES. And then appeared the face and name of the candidate.

To say publicly that one *cares* about seniors is not really to have taken a stand on an issue. You merely have let the voters know which "issues" you care about, because then they will know that those are the issues you will work on. And no one can work on them better than you, because no one else (on the ballot) is as smart as you. Such a campaign is about competence, not ideology.

The second reason that the New Elite never talks and seldom thinks about issues is that all its members share the same opinions. The partial stratification of American society by test scores has led to geographic isolation as well. It's not only that members of the New Elite talk mostly with each other—the real problem is that they don't even *know* anyone who isn't a lot like themselves.

In the olden days, say a century ago, when equality of opportunity was less abundant than now, and far less tied to test scores (less than 5 percent of the population went to college), there were neighborhoods that were markedly diverse. Not diverse ethnically or racially (we do far better today) but diverse in terms of IQ. Each neighborhood—be it Italian or Irish or Yankee or Jewish or African American—was a microcosm of the universe. In terms of ability, it was like the whole world. Some were smart and some were stupid, but most were somewhere in between. In other words, a cross section of humanity had been dumped down in a specific place.

In general, there was considerable agreement within each neighborhood because most of those who lived there were in the same economic boat. A poor neighborhood voted one way and a rich neighborhood voted another. It was *always* the economy, stupid.

But while each neighborhood voted one way, not so each city. The Italians might vote differently from the Irish, and the Jews from the WASPs. To win an election for mayor of the city, or member of Congress, you had to appeal to people of different points of view. And very often you had to compromise.

No more. Now you can have a place where everyone thinks the same. More than a city—an ideopolis. A word coined by Judis and Teixeira: ideopolis. They describe it as "postindustrial metropolis":

> A quarter or so of the jobs in Austin (Texas), Raleigh–Durham, Boston, or San Francisco are held by professionals and technicians. Plentiful, too, are low-level service and information workers, including waiters, hospital orderlies, salesclerks, janitors, and teacher's aides. Many of these jobs have been filled by Hispanics and African-Americans, just as many of the high-level professional jobs have been filled by Asian immigrants. It's one reason that the workforce in these areas we call ideopolises tend to be ethnically diverse and more complex in their stratification (various combinations of employers, employees, contract workers, temps, consultants, and the self-employed) than the workforce of the older industrial city.
>
> The ethos and mores of many of these new metropolitan areas tend to be *libertarian* and *bohemian* [emphasis added], because of the people they attract. Economists Richard Florida and Gary Gates found a close connection between the concentration of gays and of the foreign-born and the concentration of high technology and information technology within a given area. They also found a high percentage of people who identified themselves as artists, musicians, and craftspeople. Concluded Florida, "Diversity is a powerful force in the value systems and choices of the new workforce, whose members want to work for companies and live in communities that reflect their openness and tolerance. The number one factor in choosing a place to live and work, they say, is diversity. Talented people will not move to a place that ostracizes certain groups. . . ."

In the San Francisco Bay Area or the Chicago Metro area, the world and culture of the ideopolis pervades the entire metropolitan area. Many of the same people, the same businesses, and the same coffee shops or bookstores can be found in the central city or in the suburbs. These are the most advanced and integrated ideopolises. Potentially, many of these areas used to be Republican, but have become extremely Democratic in their politics. . . .

In the most advanced ideopolises, the whole working class seems to embrace the same values as professionals, and in some of them white working-class men vote remarkably similarly to their female counterparts. (73–74)

So not only are ideopolises sprouting across the land, but also they are inhabited by those who *choose* to live there for the lifestyle and tolerance. There is, of course, considerable truth in all this.

Except for one word: diversity. There is diversity of race and (to some degree) income, and of gender and sexual preference. There is even diversity of language. But there is remarkably little diversity of thought—most noticeably political thought. People in an ideopolis may think of themselves as politically independent, but they still seem to vote the same way.

In an ideopolis close to the authors' description, the San Francisco Bay Area, Congresswoman Nancy Pelosi represents a district that in 2000 favored Al Gore over George Bush by a margin of 77 percent to 15. Fifteen! That's political diversity?

What matters is not which party the district favors, but that nearly everyone votes alike. Is a district (or an ideopolis) really "diverse" if it is inhabited heavily by people who have chosen to live with others much like themselves?

The ideopolis is where the New Elite lives and works. It is not, like the immigrant neighborhoods of old, a microcosm of the universe. It is only one small aspect of that universe, numerically multiplied, a single point on the bell curve—on the downward slope to the right.

People in an ideopolis can have high incomes or low, much education or little, but most feel that they are morally and intellectually superior to the great majority of people, whom they see as a mass of dullards scattered throughout the vast and tasteless regions beyond their haven.

This sense of superiority stems from the absolute belief by the New Elite that people like themselves are smart and enlightened. This belief is absolute because their intelligence has supposedly been proven—certified by scores and rankings and diplomas. Of course, not everybody in the ideopolis is employed as a professional. But however humble their work, they don't really resemble what used to be called the proletariat. The waiters are actors, the janitors are students, the cabbies are immigrants, and those who deliver pizzas are dropouts—having dropped out only after some talent had been certified by the fact of admission, which is very different from, almost the opposite of, never having been educated at all. Actually, nearly everyone in the ideopolis is a drop-*in:* they chose to be there. And since they chose to be near smart people, they must be smart, too. (Not unlike the poor souls who like to think they're rich because they rent a small apartment in Beverly Hills.)

Aside from being smarter than everyone else, citizens of the ideopolis imagine that they're morally superior, too. And possessed of infallible good taste. This is because there is no one to contradict them. They *are* the tastemakers—in morals as well as fashion. In fact, for the new class, morality *is* a kind of fashion—you've got to keep up.

Perhaps this is why the members of the new class don't really discuss political issues, but merely list them. So long as everyone that you know agrees with you, what's the point?

Which is why the ideopolis is not the spearhead of an emerging majority but instead the incubator of electoral defeat. It's so *simple.* And everybody gets it but those superisolated smarties: *You can't win an election when you have no connection whatsoever with the majority.* If you're out of touch, you're not in office. That's how democracy works.

So danger lurks in associating only with people like yourself. While the New Elite considers itself highly "sensitive," it is in fact sensitive only to passing fads and the whining of peers. It is completely insensitive to the values and concerns and fears and hopes of the majority of its fellow citizens. This insensitivity is a harbinger not of victory but of defeat.

During the midterm election of 2002, for example, a number of Senate Democrats opposed President Bush's Homeland Security Bill, not because they felt it posed a threat to civil liberties or would lead to a massive new bureaucracy, but because it would remove some federal employees from civil service status, which was opposed by some unions. They threw this ball with unconcern, and the Republicans ran eighty yards with it. The Democrats were charged with putting special-interest group demands over national security. Fair or not, this symbol stuck. And it helped defeat Georgia senator Max Cleland, a brave patriot who had left both legs and an arm in Vietnam.

Should his Republican opponent be blamed for questioning Cleland's patriotism? Absolutely. But perhaps even greater blame should be laid at the feet of Democratic strategists, so inured from risk by gerrymander, so isolated from the citizenry by class, so untested as political advisers because all they have ever done is raise money, that they hadn't a clue as to what would fly in a campaign and what would not.

In its postelection analysis, the November 18, 2002, issue of *Time* quoted the deposed majority leader of the Senate, Democrat Tom Daschle, as saying Republicans had won because "This country is still in the upheaval of 9/11." In the same issue, Charles Krauthammer titled his full-page essay on why the Democrats lost "It's the Terrorism, Stupid."

Yes, but there's something to be said for political strategists actually seeing these things *before* an election. The American public did. The Republican party did. What about all those experts on the other side? It's not that Democrats are less concerned about national security than Republicans. Rather, the New Elite's insistence on so busily "educating" Democratic candidates has resulted in a nearly total disconnect between themselves and the public. They've unplugged the phone and replaced their windows with mirrors. They hadn't forgotten 9/11, but it lacked for them the centrality, the preemption, the enduring imminence that had seized the nation when the towers fell.

Having said this, we should note that the idea of the postelection consensus was not entirely true. While national security was paramount over other issues, it was never the *only* issue. It became the only issue when the Democrats raised no others. For example, it was difficult to find Democratic candidates even *naming* estate tax abolition as an issue. Did they think it was too complicated for the voters? A *New York Times*/CBS News poll, taken three weeks after the 2002 election, showed that Americans held favorable views of President Bush and the Republicans, even though they did not favor many of their policies.

But there is something else that helps explain the Democratic losses in 2002. It was not only the retreat from issues. It was also the absence of civility: good manners, respect for another's opinion, decorum. The perceived failure to adhere to these rules of conduct helped lose a major battle in what now could be called the "uncivil war."

Let it be said at once that the New Elite is not alone in the abandonment of civility. Right-wing talk show hosts are very often savage, intemperate, and unsparingly personal in their attacks. There is a sort of Gresham's law in political discourse today in which bad behavior has driven out the good—at least at the extremes. And in the debased and polarized politics that is a New Elite legacy there often seems to be nothing *but* extremes. Is there anything more contemptible in our national culture now than the televised "talk shows" of screaming heads—supposedly educated people shouting at one another, interrupting each interruption until no sentence is completed—and their angry bombast, infantile behavior, subhuman behavior, prehuman behavior, like the simians at the water hole in *2001: A Space Odyssey?*

Civil behavior is central to the cause of the new class war. In the 2002 election of the *Almanac of American Politics,* its lead author, Michael Barone, says that the Bush and Gore voters represent "two nations of different faiths. One is observant, tradition-minded, moralistic; the other is unobservant, liberation-minded, relativist." (Judis and Teixeira are fair enough to quote this in their book, albeit under the heading "Tenuous Case for a Republican Majority.") Barone even claims that "demography is moving, slowly, toward the Bush nation."

Now what role does civility play in the battle for ascendancy between "two nations," the Red and the Blue? It tips the balance. It may be the most important weight on the scale.

Civility is the key to which side of the fence one is on. If one is "unobservant, liberation-minded, relativist," then the only restraint on one's behavior is law. If one is "observant, tradition-minded, moralistic," then one is bound primarily by rules. Unlike laws, civility is a rule and rules are self-enforced. This distinction now divides the nation.

The most memorable and dramatic incident in the 2002 campaign shows how explosive that division has become. Ten days before the election, a twin-engine plane crashed in a forest in northern Minnesota, killing all eight passengers, including Democratic senator Paul Wellstone, his wife, Sheila, and their daughter. People were stunned. Many who had never met Wellstone, had never voted for him, and had strongly opposed his views said silent prayers or crossed themselves, or blew their noses to conceal their grief. The reaction was universal: what a terrible tragedy, what a terrible loss, may God rest their souls.

The state wasn't *plunged* into grief, it *rose* to a level of grief in which partisanship was no factor.

Of course, the clock was ticking and the election near. The Democrats hurriedly asked former vice president Walter Mondale to replace Wellstone on the ticket, and though very comfortably situated at age seventy-four, he graciously complied.

The polls showed that Mondale would win. There was an enormous wave of sympathy for Wellstone and a natural desire among many to continue his legacy. It is important to note that at the time of his death, Wellstone also had been leading in the polls, even though he had voted against authorizing war against Iraq (or perhaps *because* he had). He was the only Democratic senator in a close race who had not supported it. Despite the bill's popularity, his approval ratings immediately rose. There is a moral to this: you are better off voting against the majority on clear principle than in ducking the issue and standing for nothing.

Wellstone's whole career was much misunderstood. To the Washington insiders, he had the most liberal voting record in the Senate, perhaps in Senate history. But to Minnesota voters, he was not so much a liberal as a populist. He was more like a 1930s radical than a 1960s protester.

He was certainly not a member of the New Elite. Though a college professor, he seemed more like the wrestling coach he also was. While members of the New Elite adored him, so did miners on the Iron Range. He had strong blue-collar appeal. His personal enemy wasn't the masses, it was the rich. Though not really a member of the New Elite, he was a tireless foe of the old elite.

With Mondale holding high aloft Wellstone's banner, it seemed that the election would be merely a formality. Yet he lost, receiving barely 48 percent of the vote. Though perhaps the most respected public figure in the state, he lost the election.

The reversal began at a memorial service. On October 29, one week before the election, those close to Wellstone and the Democratic–Farmer–Labor Party of Minnesota thought they should stage an event that everyone would remember. The day before, there had been a traditional funeral at a Minneapolis synagogue for the Wellstone family and close friends. It had been dignified and traditional.

But now it was time for a *memorial service.* What the planners had in mind should have been clear from their selection of a forum—the mammoth basketball arena at the University of Minnesota. It had twenty thousand seats, and all were filled hours before the service. That's what it was called—the "service." And so many wanted to participate in this "service," which *sounded* funereal, that all the local television stations were broadcasting it live. A clear majority of Minnesotans had tuned in.

Three hours later, of course, they had completely tuned out. Why they did so has become a national legend.

But the legend is not quite right. It focuses on a grieving friend of Wellstone, the most destructive Khan since Genghis, who got up and made a spectacularly weird and partisan speech.

Still, it was but a single shot in this new uncivil war. It was the *rest* of the memorial service that actually did the trick.

For one thing, it should never have been held in a basketball arena. One of the reasons that it looked like a political convention is there are no concession stands at most memorial services. At any given moment, there were thousands of people at the back of the hall, eating and drinking, slapping and hugging, trading stories and in general doing everything but dropping balloons. Some of the more tradition-minded viewers must have thought they had the wrong channel, but there *was* no other channel; unless you had cable, they were all the same.

There were other problems. High-fiving someone at a memorial isn't civil behavior, especially if you're a former president of the United States on camera. And it's *really* uncivil to insult your fellow mourners. When Trent Lott was introduced and very loudly booed, the viewing audience was shocked. They were also startled to learn that Vice President Cheney had been quite publicly disinvited. The problem wasn't that it was so partisan, but that it was so hostile. When Jesse Ventura walks out of a cacophonic arena in disgust, you know you're very far away indeed from civil.

Writing soon after in the *Wall Street Journal,* Michael Barone was reminded of the booing of Nelson Rockefeller at the Republican National Convention in 1964: "The vitriolic cast of the opposition helped Kennedy and his successor LBJ to raise their party's standing up from parity toward their high job ratings. The vitriolic cast of Mr. Bush's opposition could lead to the same kind of rallying to the President's party by the large section of the electorate that didn't vote for him in 2000 but now approves of his performance." It's the civility, stupid.

It wasn't that those repelled by incivility had nowhere else to go. There was George Bush, who through ubiquity had nationalized the election. He made himself, not his party, the real opposition, then he practically made a cult of civility. No sooner had Bush moved into the White House than rules (not laws) of conduct were decreed. There was a dress code. Infighting among the staff (which is to Washington what soccer is to Liverpool) would cease. Everyone was to be polite, prompt, and soft-spoken. The apex of the pyramid was an embodiment of self-control who had quit drinking in his forties and was in bed each night by nine-thirty or ten. George Bush was so dignified that only good humor and cowboy boots kept him from seeming stuffy; and since he seemed to be in every state at once, most decidedly in Minnesota just before the election, there was an observably civil harbor for all those craft in flight from stormy seas.

But can we really say it's the *Republican* Party that's emerging just now? Especially in the face of all those Democratic demographics? The truth is that the emerging majority *is* the majority. It's whichever party seems most in favor of majority rule and appeals most widely to the majority of voters. The way to lose an election is to imply that *we* know what's best for *you*. The public always votes against the *we*.

This book has tried to show why the Democrats, if encumbered by New Elite myopia and hauteur, will continue to lose. But it could just as easily be the Republicans. If events in Iraq go neither as desired nor as predicted, if the economy does not merely sour but sinks, if party dominance leads to zealotry (as in the Gingrich years), if political control prompts litmus tests offensive to the majority, if the challenger seems clearly more in touch with the people than does the incumbant, then it may well be that the Democrats will reemerge.

But Democrats will not prevail so long as their wagon is hitched solely to the ideopolis's star. Elitism is a weight that keeps the pendulum from swinging back, and hatred of the new class may be a weight even heavier than resentment of our old elite.

The ideopolises are indeed responsible for the blue in the red and blue electoral maps. But how long will even that last? The immigrants, the Hispanics, the members of the working class who still make things are part of the ideopolis, too, perhaps most of it, though largely unseen by the new class that lives in another part of town. These groups are tradition-minded, too, and find that a life with rules may be freer than one with no moral compass.

So long as tradition is the enemy of tolerance, it will have no broad appeal. But if a nation can grow more tolerant and more respectful of difference, as America in recent decades clearly has, then tradition becomes the framework for growth. What people want—what one side feels is bred in our bones and even the other admits is in our DNA—is community.

Community is more urgently needed now than when Neanderthals huddled together for safety. The disorientation of increasingly rapid change is more to be feared than the tiger's roar. Community permits us to make the voyage in peace.

Reds and blues are for election maps. A nation that is also a community needs no such demarcation. As issues and circumstances change, so will the outcomes of elections. Politically, the majority will change over time, as it always has. But belief in the majority must never be abandoned. And those who would do so will never be emergent in power, or entitled to it, or worthy to address our common needs and ancient prayers.

About the Author

David Lebedoff was born and raised in Minneapolis, where he currently lives with his wife and three children. He is a graduate of the University of Minnesota and the Harvard Law School and the author of five books, including the prize-winning *Cleaning Up* (Free Press).

An earlier book, *The New Elite* (Franklin Watts), which began as an article in *Esquire*, was the precursor to *The Uncivil War*. It described the growth of a new class and what its effects on our society were likely to be. The *National Review* called *The New Elite* "a tremendous work, radiant with intelligence.... In his precision and lucidity, [Lebedoff] is a latter-day Tocqueville."

The Uncivil War is the story of a nightmare come true. Lebedoff's earlier predictions have unfortunately come to pass, in ways that are all too recognizable.